Following My Bliss

Following My Bliss

a memoir

Sallie Hanna-Rhyne

REGENT PRESS
Berkeley, California

ISBN 13: 978-1-58790-589-6

ISBN 10: 1-58790-589-2

Library of Congress Cataloging In Publication: 2021951506

Cover Design: Paul Veres

Printed in the U.S.A.

REGENT PRESS
Berkeley, California
www.regentpress.net

This book is dedicated to my parents,
to Mother and Daddy
in whose hands I experienced
a blissful early childhood.

In the beginning of heaven and earth there were no words
Words came out of the womb of matter;
And whether you dispassionately see to the core of life
Or passionately see the surface
The core and the surface are essentially the same,
Words making them seem different
Only to express appearances.
If name be needed, wonder names them both:
From wonder to wonder
Existence opens

The Way of Life by Lao Tzu
Translated by Witter Bynner 1944

Table of Contents

BROOKLYN

Daddy and Sallie, Prospect Park, 1939

Beginnings

"I had kinda hoped for a boy but two days of Sallie Ann cured that, and I wouldn't sell 'my half' for a million," so wrote my dad in a letter to his sister, Adalene, after I was born on May 12th, 1939. Daddy and Aunt Nene were part of a large, close-knit Southern family. She lived near Huntsville in Jeff, Alabama.

Mother was equally thrilled with her offspring. Our old family photographs show her as a beaming and adoring young mother with her smiling baby at Prospect Park in Brooklyn, New York, and in Alabama with Daddy's family. It was summertime, hot, and in both Brooklyn and Alabama, we spent a lot of time outdoors.

Mother was thirty-four years old and Daddy was thirty-five, older parents for the time. The old photos show my handsome parents in stylish outfits: Mother had a cape-like coat and a wide-brimmed hat; Daddy wore his hat at a rakish angle; and in one photo at Coney Island, Mother wore slacks—very unconventional for a woman in 1939.

Mother breast-fed her children. This was not the norm in 1939, 1941 or 1947 when her children were born. Doctors, as well as the media, encouraged women to use infant formula rather than breast-feed. Maybe because my mother was born in Scotland, she believed in old-fashioned ways. I was the happy recipient of my mother's milk and my mother's love.

We lived in the Park Slope area of Brooklyn, a decent working-class neighborhood near Prospect Park. Park Slope offered endless outdoor opportunities to families with young children. Prospect Park, Brooklyn's jewel, was comparable to Central Park

Mother and Sallie, Prospect Park, 1939

Friend, Mother, Rebel, Fred in carriage 1941, Prospect Park.

in Manhattan. When we were babes and toddlers, Mother took us to the park in our baby carriages. She commented in her diary that taking her children to the park and watching them grow was the best time of her life.

Our family picnicked in the park, sitting on a blanket on the grass, soaking up the sun, and eating together. All the neighborhood children played in the playground area on the swings, the slides, and the monkey bars. When we were older, we skated and biked on the smooth paths, and on winter days, we sledded down the snowy hills. Brooklyn was a city and part of the city of New York, but we also knew the joys of trees, grass, and meadows. The meadows in Prospect Park were large green swaths, and we called them "First Meadow and "Second Meadow."

My brother Fred was born in 1941, another happy occasion for my parents. Now I had a baby brother! I must have been jealous of Fred taking up the space I previously had to myself in my parents' attention. The Oedipus and Electra complexes developed early in my family: I was in love with my dad, and Fred drew closer with Mother. I can see these trends in the photos of that time. There was a story in my family about the day Daddy entered the living room to greet guests, but before he could say hello, I rushed to him and exclaimed, "Daddy you shaved your moustache!" I was the first in the family to recognize the difference in my daddy's appearance.

When the United States entered the War, a huge change came for everyone in Park Slope. We used food ration books and tokens. We recycled. There were blackouts. The blackouts were fun for us, the young children. We knew something was up, but we were not informed of the danger, so we were not fearful. We hid under the table when the lights were out, and the curtains were drawn. We giggled and enjoyed what we considered a game. Daddy was too old for the draft, but he volunteered at the local hospitals. Mother had her hands full with housekeeping and two young children.

The community feeling in the neighborhood was strong, intensified by the War. People felt patriotic, and we all loved our president, Franklin Roosevelt. We were happy to ration food and recycle—it was our duty. We saved newspapers, metal, and the tinfoil on chewing gum wrappers that we peeled off and balled up to donate. Women even saved the fat trimmings from meat in tin cans. There was a sign at Mr. Kintzberger's butcher shop on 8th Avenue that read: Ladies bring your fat cans in on Tuesday.

My brother Fred and I were very conscious of the end

of the War. I was six; Fred was four. The celebrations were numerous. Nightly, people would burn effigies of Hitler and Tojo on lampposts then roast potatoes in bonfires on the street. The police were tolerant of these fires. The community had block parties that brought everyone out on the street, sharing food and stories. There was a general euphoria now that the long ordeal was over. There is a picture of me leading a group of children in a daytime impromptu parade. I am carrying a baton, wearing a spangly costume, and tap shoes. I had just started tap dance lessons at Retta's Dance Studio, so I had the perfect fancy outfit.

I loved the dance lessons at Retta's. I was one of eight girls called the "Powder Puff Dollies," a group of six or seven year olds who performed at a dance recital that year. We smiled sweetly in our white tutus, soft white hats, and tap shoes with big bows. My dear friend, Ann, was there with me too.

At the same time, I also began piano lessons. We had a venerable, old, upright piano that my father's sister, Aunt Janet, played when she visited. Now, I was learning how to play it, and I loved it. Mr. Doxy, a very kind and gentle person came to our home once a week to instruct me. After one year of piano and tap lessons, Mother told me that I needed to choose between the two activities. I chose piano, but all through my childhood, adolescence, and adulthood, dancing has always brought me great joy.

After the War, I remember a map of Europe pinned up on our kitchen cabinet. It was a map that showed the countries usurped by the Soviet Union after the cessation of hostilities. I was a bit fearful of that red-creeping color over the map, but my parents assured me that we were safe in the United States, an ocean away from Europe.

The concept of the Iron Curtain was strongly imprinted on my mind in the 1940s. It wasn't until 1961, when I went to Poland with my friend Lynda that I realized for much of my childhood, I didn't think the sun shone in Poland, because it was behind the Iron Curtain. I believe children are very susceptible to images like that. I had no idea that the concept of the Iron Curtain had been buried in my consciousness for all that time.

In 1947, Fred and I knew our mother was pregnant because we could feel the baby moving inside her belly. After some time an unusual thing happened; our parents woke us up in the middle of the night and told us we would have to be alone for a little while because Daddy was taking Mother to the hospital to have the baby. Fred and I sat together on the lower bunk bed and sang "Happy Birthday" to our new sibling. It was a joyous occasion when Billy, the beloved baby of the family, came into our lives.

Fred, Sallie, Billy Prospect Park 1947.

The Sidewalks of New York

By the time I was eight I was going out to play by myself, (i.e., without my mother). But, I was never by myself. The sidewalks of New York were alive with children playing: bouncing balls, hitting balls with a broomstick-pole, running the bases, kicking-the-can in the air, hopping the potsy grid, jumping rope, and playing cards on the stoops. The air was pulsing with energy, throbbing with the vitality of children's physical play. We were totally in the moment; we all felt we had to keep up with these Brooklyn street games—it was a child's paradise.

The girls' games combined physicality with literacy. Our games used the alphabet, names of places, and names of people with the coordination of bouncing a ball under your leg on the correct first letter.

"A. My name is Anna and my husband's name is Al.

We come from Alabama and we sell apples."

We bounced the ball under our legs on all the A words including "and" then continued through the alphabet. The ball bouncer and the girls waiting for a turn had to be focused, so they could catch a mistake, and then they could take their turn.

"I Took a Trip Around the World" was a similar but even more challenging game.

The ball was bounced under your leg, back and forth, on all the places we could name in alphabetical order. We ended with W as we didn't know any places starting with X. The game had two more parts: "These Are the Girls I Met," and "These Are the Boys I Met." I still have these lists in the back of my mind; we worked hard to memorize them. Twenty-three times bouncing the ball back and forth under your legs while reciting the names was no small feat for a young girl. And it was fun!

Our version of hopscotch was called "Potsy." We chalked the grid on the sidewalk, numbers one through ten ending with a semicircle we called "Honeymoon," the turnaround spot. We used rocks or bottle caps to throw onto the numbered squares to mark our place.

We also loved to jump rope. There were many jump rope rhymes, like:

"I had a little brother his name was Tiny Tim,
I put him in the bathtub to teach him how to swim,
He drank all the water; he ate all the soap,
He died last night with a bubble in his throat.
In came the doctor, in came the nurse, in came the lady with the alligator purse.
Out went the doctor, out went the nurse, out went the lady with the alligator purse."

One time, my best friend Ann was turning the rope with another girl for me to jump, and Ann deliberately pulled the rope so I would trip. I ran into the vestibule of our apartment house and cried tears all alone on the steps. I felt the injustice of Ann's move, but since I felt that she had more personal power than I did, I could do nothing about it. I was too timid to confront her, and I never even thought of going upstairs to tell my mother. We played on the street unsupervised. Occasionally a mom would lean out of a window and peer around, but grown-ups were not involved in our play. We children dealt with these conflicts ourselves. The boys might duke it out with their fists, the girls would yell or cry and then get over it. We all wanted to play, and these issues were just minor setbacks.

Ann was the leader of our girl group, and no one questioned her authority. She was in charge; she took the reins and we followed her. She was also the best player, so who would challenge her right to be captain in a team game? She wouldn't play unless she was the captain, and we all wanted to play, so Ann was always captain. Years later when I studied astrology, I remembered Ann's birthday: August 3rd. She was a Leo sun sign. She was indeed the leading player on the stage of our street theater. We were attracted to her and the glow she had about her; she wanted the limelight, and we didn't. The other aspects of Leo were in her personality too. She was a generous and loving friend and intensely loyal. I think she thought of me as her pet. I was smaller, shorter, thinner, and even more fragile to her more chunky physique. I was also a year younger and a Protestant. That was deficient, even defective by her strong, vigorous Catholic standards.

Park Slope was not the gentrified area of today but an average working-class neighborhood. We had a silly saying, "I'm from Park Slop, I mean Slope." That was more word play than description. Our environs were not slummy, but neither were they fancy. Daddy was a skilled worker, a telephone installer for AT&T. That good job enabled us to live on 11th Street near the park. Our entrance to Prospect Park was marked by a three-foot stonewall where you could sit and swing your legs and watch the world go by on the park side. The playground inside the park was fenced in for young children. We exulted in swinging, sliding, and climbing the monkey bars with no protective garb—no padding under play structures in those days—we fell and skinned our knees, got up, ran and played some more. We bumped our heads, broke bones and sometimes had stitches. We lived and played to the fullest, and we took the hard knocks in stride.

Outside the playground was Prospect Park's band shell, a large elevated stage and a smooth, paved area for dancing. Big bands played for social dancing on Friday nights in the summer. On Wednesday evenings country bands played for square dancing. I remember walking up to the park at night with my family and there would be hundreds of people taking part in these community dances. I watched the grownups at the social dances, and I participated in the square dancing. The large circular area in front of the bandstand was filled with squares of four couples, swinging their partners: do-si-doeing and grand marching. I was a young girl after the War; to me it was exciting and lots of fun.

Sallie, Marcella, Elaine — Prospect Park 1946

Roller-skating was very much a part of my childhood in Brooklyn. I was seven years old in 1946 when my roller skating phase began, and it lasted until I was about twelve years old. Because our play was very physical, I would come home from school and change from a dress or a skirt into my dungarees (jeans) then I would go out to play. We had metal skates with metal wheels. The skates clipped onto our shoes with a metal clasp that we tightened with a skate key. The clasps were small and fitted onto the edges of our shoes. More expensive skates had wider clasps that encompassed more of your shoe; we never had expensive skates. Our skates had a leather strap that went around your ankle. We wore the skate key around our necks on a string. The key lengthened or shortened our skates to accommodate different shoes and the growth of our feet.

Skating on the smooth street surface was easier and more enjoyable than the bumpy sidewalk. Luckily there were not many cars on our street in the 1940s. The park had many smooth pathways to skate and gentle hills to climb and glide down. We raced around on our skates feeling the wind pulse through our bodies and the glory of free movement.

The metal wheels eventually wore out, and little holes appeared. We called them "skellies." Boys would take the old wheels and attach them to wooden crates to make scooters. This was exclusively a boy project— boys knew about tools, hammers, nails, nuts and bolts—girls were not interested.

Recently my brother Fred supplied me with the following information: A wooden crate could be procured at the corner grocery store and a two-by-four needed to be found. The old roller skate wheels were attached to the crate along with the two-by-four as a running board for one foot, the other leg and foot pushed. The boys would remove the rubber from the wheels of the skates for the front of the scooter. The rubber cushioned the skates and prevented too sharp of a turn when roller-skating, but without rubber, the scooter could turn quickly and take off easily. Savvy boys would extend the running board beyond the front of the crate and use an old shoe heel for a bumper! I never noticed these details. Fred also mentioned that handlebars were getting a little too fancy, and no boy wanted his friends to think his dad had helped him. Independence and autonomy among children was cherished. We wanted to do things on our own from an early age, and we never saw a store-bought scooter in our neighborhood.

Once we became teenagers, we no longer skated on the street. We went to a roller-skating rink and rented shoe-skates with wooden wheels. Recorded music of the day played as we rolled around the elliptical rink. We skated effortlessly on the wood floor; we felt graceful as we slipped along. We always travelled together in groups of five or ten. At the rink, girls often held hands and skated in twos, threes or fours. Boy-girl couples were starting to form, and these couples skated together romantically. It was easy to control speed on these skates, and I felt weightless as I floated around the rink.

One girl in our crowd of friends, Peggy Healey, was an exceptional skater. She joined a Roller Derby team in Brooklyn. This was a rough sport, and the promoters encouraged the girls to push each other and act nasty to the other team. Peggy did not do that the night we went

Sallie, Mother, Fred, Rebel — Prospect Park 1946

to her game. She skated strongly, and she used her speed and agility to move past the other team on the track.

My friends and I also ice skated in those days of yore. In the winter, a red flag was posted on the Lafayette Monument at one entrance to the park. The flag was to let people know when the lake was frozen and ready for skaters. This too was a group activity for friends and families to skate together outdoors. I was thrilled when I got "figure" skates one year for Christmas. It was more difficult than roller-skating but just as rewarding when you found your groove and whooshed around the lake with savoir-faire.

Park Slope

In the 1940s and up until 1956, our family lived on 11th Street in Park Slope. It was mostly an Irish-Catholic, working-class neighborhood where the streets sloped down along with the income levels. Our family paid forty-eight dollars a month for a four-room apartment in a sixteen-unit white-stone building. We lived in one of the many rent-controlled apartments, and I remember Mr. Toner, a tall, official looking man in a suit, who came to collect our monthly rent.

The front door to our building was made of glass and wrought iron, and it opened to a large vestibule where young children could escape the mob of their peers. This was a place where we could laugh, cry, or brood alone. Teenage girls would practice dance steps here, and teenage couples stole kisses in this protected place.

Up from the vestibule was another heavy, glass door that led to the hallway; it was always locked. Behind this door was a staircase connecting the floors that had four apartments on each level. Behind the first staircase was an open space with no access to the street, and that was a scary place for me. I always ran lickety-split by that space, up the stairs to our apartment on the second floor. Once, I had a nightmare that a crazy man was after me in the hallway just beyond that scary place: as I mounted the stairs, my legs turned to stone, and I couldn't move. I woke up in a sweat. That space always gave me an eerie feeling.

All the apartments in our building had the same layout, and the apartments across the hall were the mirror image. The front door opened to a hall and there was a bathroom on the right. A few more steps, also on the right was a bedroom, the only bedroom with a door. And at the end of the hall was the living room at a right angle to the hall. Mother and Daddy's bedroom was connected by sliding doors to the living room, and the kitchen was past their room. There was also a small hall connecting the larger hall to the kitchen bypassing the living room. After our family became five people and, we had lived in our apartment over ten years, the small hall became a storeroom and filled up with boxes. My brothers and I accumulated many things over time: bicycles, roller skates, ice skates, sleds, scooters, electric trains on a large board, and a doll house handmade by Daddy. My brothers and I used all these items at different times of the year.

Mother and Daddy's bedroom and the living room had two windows that looked out to the back of the 12th Street apartments. We could look down from these windows and see the superintendent's patio and their many potted plants. Mr. and Mrs. Cole, the supers, had a parrot, and in the summertime, Polly the parrot's cage was outside. She would sit on her perch outside the cage squawking the traditional "Polly wants a cracker."

Mr. and Mrs. Cole were Jamaican, the only black people living on our street. They lived behind the coal cellar in the basement. We would walk by the giant pile of coal to knock on their door. They were very nice people, and one of their jobs was to ignite the coal furnace to provide the steam heat we enjoyed in the winter. Sometimes in the morning the heat would be late, and people would bang on the radiators to show their discomfort; New York could be frigid on winter mornings. On Saturdays, we were sometimes awakened by the coal truck sending its wares noisily down a chute into the cellar.

Mr. Cole also collected the garbage. There was a dumbwaiter in each apartment, a shaft with a pulley system that sent up a shelf for us to put our garbage bag on. Mr. Cole would slap the rope on the dumbwaiter door when the shelf was at the apartment level. "P.U.," my brother Fred would say when he opened the door to put our garbage out. The shaft was dirty and smelly and allowed the spread of roaches throughout the building.

A refrigerator replaced the icebox of the earlier days, and we had a washing machine with a hand-cranked wringer. Outside our kitchen window was a clothesline. In fair weather mother hung our laundry out to dry. In foul weather, she used a contraption that let down from the kitchen ceiling. She would hang clothes on wooden slats and then pull it up to the ceiling so the clothes could dry. The kitchen window also looked down on the alleyway. In the summers, mellifluous Italian tenors would come into the alleyway and sing beautiful arias for the pennies the tenants would toss from the windows. What a treat!

My brother Fred and I shared a bedroom, and although Mother closed our door every night, it did not block out our parents' arguing, fighting, and yelling. Once when Daddy had been drinking, the squabbling was noisy enough that Fred and I pressed our ears up against our closed door to listen. Daddy knocked over a freestanding wardrobe, and Fred and I burst out of our room at the loud sound. "See Fred," Mother said to Daddy, "I told you the children would hear you." She was upset, but she covered it up. She assured us that everything was all right, and told us to go back to bed.

When Billy graduated from his crib next to my

mother, he moved into the bedroom with Fred and me—now there were three of us in one room! It was crowded with a single bed, a bunk bed, two dressers, and a table. The one built-in closet was also in this room. Packed with clothing for five people (for both hot and cold weather) and various old toys, the built-in closet was a fun place to hide during rainy day games.

All the tenant families in our apartment house knew each other. Marcella Moran was in apartment #1, and Eleanor Conklin lived in apartment #2. We visited each other and played outside together. Eleanor's family had a big English sheep dog with long hair covering his eyes. He was loved by all. My family was on the second floor, apartment #7, and we too had a dog. Rebel was a small fox terrier we inherited from Aunt Janet. On the third floor was my dear friend, Ann, her two brothers, and parents. Miss Petri lived next door to their family. We blamed Miss Petri, an elderly spinster who liked to bake, for the spread of roaches, because we thought she did not clean up properly. The truth was, no one was fastidious and roaches were ubiquitous. We used pesticides, but it was hopeless. We would squeal when we turned the bathroom light on, and the roaches scattered.

Jeanne Cronin lived on the fourth floor, but she died young from a rare disease. All the families in the building attended her wake, and although we felt sad about her death, the children ended up giggling and wiggling around. We were not reproached; the grownups knew that death was not real to us children.

There was roof access from the fourth floor, and as I grew older, the roof was a place for clandestine activities like smoking. I would snitch a few cigarettes from my dad's pack of Pall Malls, sneak up to the roof; Ann and I would puff the forbidden tobacco. We girls had gabfests on the roof, telling secrets and eventually our opinions of the boys we knew.

Ann's elderly aunt came from Ireland to live with her family, and she made their living space even more crowded. Ann's older brother, Jackie, would tease their Aunt Margaret mercilessly when their parents were not at home. Aunt Margaret was formidable, tall, and large boned. Mostly she sat in her chair quietly, but every so often Jackie's piercing taunts drove her to the edge. She would rise from her chair and chase Jackie shouting, "You bold, brazen blackguard!" Ann and I would hide our faces and laugh.

After the War, working class families in our neighborhood earned good wages, but no one spent a lot of money. Layaways or buying on credit was not our way. Mother and Daddy would save money and pay cash for large items such as a television set. We got ours in 1949 when I was ten. I tried watching it, but "Howdy Doody" was not my cup of tea. I liked the mystery movies we watched at Elaine's house across the street. She would invite a bunch of kids over to watch these spooky stories. Later my family watched "Your Show of Shows" together. We all laughed at the antics of Sid Caesar and Imogene Coca. Nonetheless, television was always secondary to me; I preferred playing outside, reading a book, or going to the soda parlor with my friends.

Our livingroom was furnished simply with a secondhand couch, an easy chair, a rug, an upright piano, and the "expensive" table. We were not allowed to do homework or color or paste on this table. It was only for dinners with company. When I was ten or so, I realized the name of that table meant that a large sum of money had been used to buy it. That was a small epiphany for me.

In 1956, when I was seventeen, Mother and Daddy bought a four-story brownstone house on 4th Street for $14,500. Mrs. Farrant, the next-door neighbor, held the note and my parents made payments to her. This was a momentous move for our family. I finally had my own room, and Fred and Bill shared a large room. This was a dramatic difference from five people and one dog sharing four rooms. There were two small apartments on the fourth floor and two other rooms that were rented out to help with mortgage payments. There was also a small backyard; at last Daddy had a space for gardening. We were amazed at his talent for growing roses, zinnias, and tomatoes. I was a freshman at Brooklyn College, and although I loved these changes, I didn't pay too much attention to them. By this time, I was college student and thoroughly immersed in my studies.

Public School, 1944-1956

P.S. 107 was three blocks away from our apartment, our neighborhood public school. I don't remember kindergarten, but I do remember first grade with Miss Houston. Mother told me that one time, Miss Houston gave our class the assignment of finding out our parents' ages. I came back with the news that my mother was eighteen and my dad was eighty! Mother had a sense of humor.

At age five, I was reading and enjoying books very much. Mother and Daddy were readers, and they read to my brothers and me. My favorite book was Alice in Wonderland. The adventures and the crazy characters were a great source of pleasure for me.

Miss Dougherty, another lovely woman, was my second grade teacher. Mid-year, however, I was promoted to the third grade. I vividly remember walking into Mrs. Swan's classroom, knowing no one and feeling very shy. I saw a bookshelf with an inviting display, so I went there to browse. A very sweet girl in the class came over to talk to me. She pointed out a book she liked that had a camel on the cover, and that was the start of a beautiful friendship with Katy Kean. We were close friends until we graduated from high school. After high school, she married a neighborhood boy, I went to college, and we eventually lost touch.

Fourth grade brought me to Mrs. Ott's class. Mrs. Ott was another exemplary and kind teacher. By this time mother was involved in the Parent Teacher Association (PTA) and over the years, she was PTA president many times. Mother had become friends with the principal of P.S. 107, Mrs. De Gemma. Later when my brother

Marcella, Sallie, PS 107 1946

Bill was at the school, Mrs. De Gemma hung one of Bill's kindergarten finger paintings in her office. Mother called it "Souls in Purgatory."

When I entered the fifth grade, I was in for a shock. Miss Conlon was my teacher, and she was different: sarcastic, mean, and strict. On the first day of class, I was directed to sit in the first row, first seat. I don't know why exactly, but maybe because my grades were good, or because I was short, but I was putting away my books when Miss Conlon asked me a question. I was not ready with the answer, and I don't even think I heard the question. She immediately moved me to a back seat. At this time, my eyesight was also changing. I was becoming nearsighted. The blackboard was getting blurrier and blurrier. I was too shy to say anything, especially to such an ogre of a teacher. One day she called on me to read something on the blackboard. Squinting my eyes, I had to admit I couldn't see it. Miss Conlon asked the class in an annoyed tone of voice, "What does she need, class?"

"Glasses," was chanted back in the singsong rhythm of child-speak.

I felt humiliated and cried silent tears. When I went home for lunch I told my mother what happened, and how I felt. Mother walked me back to school, and took Miss Conlon to task.

"You will not ever speak to my child like that again!" Mother said.

Like a lion defending her cub, my mother defended her child fiercely, and Miss Conlon never singled me out again. I also got glasses to correct my vision. My faith in good teachers was restored in the sixth grade. Miss Clark was a kind and gentle person.

Our neighborhood junior high was a bit further from my home but still within walking distance. This school is where we had our first male teachers: Mr. Weiner and Mr. Schuster. They were genial and benign people and trusted us to be on our own sometimes. Mr. Weiner would take a break for a few minutes in the teacher's lounge nearby our classroom while we did deskwork. There were some older boys in the class who had been held back, but no one was disruptive when the teacher was not in the room. I think we were proud to be trusted and behaved accordingly.

In the second year of junior high, an older boy committed a terrible crime. It happened at night close to the school grounds. This boy taunted an older man who had been drinking and had fallen down. The boy kicked the man and stomped on his body and killed him. It was shocking, horrific, and strangely intriguing to us, the younger teenagers. The boy was arrested and jailed. At school, even for those of us who were completely non-violent, there was a fascination with this boy. He had stepped over a line. He had defied the mores of the culture; he committed murder! Most of us could not even imagine the deed and would have been horrified to have seen it. Nonetheless, by this deed the boy had brought a certain significance to the school.

It was 1951 and neighborhood gangs were forming all over the city. We heard of the Tigers, a boy gang, and the Tigerettes, their girlfriends. Our crowd of teenagers was somewhat rebellious. We did not want to follow adult dictums submissively, but we were not violent or destructive.

* * *

At this time in my life the music of Chuck Berry started to filter into my listening experience. The radio brought his infectious music into our lives. Something was happening here and we loved it! We tuned into WNJR, a New Jersey station that played rhythm and blues and the rock 'n' roll of Berry and others. I remember doing my homework with this music blaring from the radio. We also listened to radio programs: Tom Mix, The Shadow, The Lone Ranger, and Superman. The Life of Riley was a funny show with a character named, Digger O'Dell, the friendly undertaker. I found that very amusing. Henry Aldrich was a teenage program. His mother would call, "Hennnnry, Henry Aldrich!" and he would reply, "Coming mother."

We read comic books: Archie, Wonder Woman, Superman, The Tales of the Crypt, and my parents had no objections. I read books and did well in school. There was, however, a book my mother objected to called, *Katherine.* It concerned a young woman who had affairs with English royalty in in the 14th century. I read this book in the sixth grade, and I had no idea what was going on. What was an affair? There were no graphic descriptions of sex, but my mother was furious. She went to the school librarian and demanded to know why this book was made available to eleven-year-olds. "This is not appropriate reading material for young children," she berated the librarian.

A year or so later, when my sexuality was developing, I read *The Amboy Dukes.* I was showing it to a friend in the bedroom that I shared with my brothers. Mother walked in, and I shoved the book behind the bed. Mother noticed and demanded to see the book. She looked it over and determined that I would return it to the public library right away. I did not understand sex or the new stirrings in my body. The information I got from my girlfriends was insufficient and sparse. When Mother tried to tell me about menstruation, I was alienated from her. "Oh, I know all that." I said. I did not. Mother did not pursue the subject, and at age thirteen, when I did get my period, she of course helped me. She purchased the pads and the belt and was sympathetic. Happily my girlfriends referred to the menses as "my friend" rather than "the curse." I still did not understand the biology, but I accepted my fate as a girl and was happy to be growing up.

In 1952, I entered Bay Ridge High School, an all girl academic public school. I loved reading and learning, so I chose this school over Manual Training High School, a vocational school closer to home. At Bay Ridge, we were prepped to go to college; math, science, and the liberal arts were challenging courses and required good attention in class and at home with our homework. The girls I met were serious students but like me wanted to have fun as well. We laughed and joked, and we sometimes cavorted about outside campus.

At one point, I was known as "Sallie, the salamander killer." My science teacher, Mrs. Neivert, was truly an inspiration. She encouraged all her students to pursue a career in science. The experiment I was doing included the care of two groups of salamanders. One group received a thyroid supplement, and the other group did not. After a few weeks of feeding the amphibians and cleaning their terrariums, I got lazy. Instead of removing the salamanders to another bowl, I cupped them in my hand while emptying their old water. Whoops! One slipped away from my hand and down the drain. I was horrified and went running down the stairs to the see a custodian. I poured out my tale of woe to this man. "Nothing can be done," he said sadly, "That salamander is already out to sea."

"Oh dear," I thought, "I'm so sorry."

Several other salamanders died of something or other. The experiment was over, and I had a new nickname.

At my all girl school, I could excel in my studies without embarrassment in front of boys who might find that unattractive. The boys I liked were in my neighborhood, and we didn't talk about books or science. Later when I was in college I met Pete Hamill, an older boy in the neighborhood who was a reporter with the New York Post, a liberal, intelligent paper at the time. Pete was a wonder to me, a neighborhood boy who read books?! Pete went on to write books and became a well-known author. We wrote letters when he was attending Mexico City College; his letters were humorous and descriptive, and they had little drawings in the margins.

At Bay Ridge High School, I met many girls of different backgrounds: Italian, Greek, Norwegian and one African-American. These students were beautiful, smart, outspoken and funny. Alba Beneforte was a tall, dark, attractive girl who stood out in a crowd with her wit, her fashionable outfits, and her short pixie haircut. She was a strong young woman. Barbara Murillo was devoted to a career as a writer. She was pretty and slender. She had a melancholy cast like a tragic heroine, maybe because she had had polio as a child and walked with a slight limp. Vicky Pappas was an energetic, down-home, natural leader. She was a star in our science classes, and one time, she led us on a crazy romp around the campus to celebrate our coming graduation.

Baseball Fever

In Brooklyn we were passionate about the things we believed were ours. The Brooklyn Eagle was our daily newspaper. Some things were basic to us as Brooklynites. We loved baseball. The boys played stick-ball on the street. Girls and boys played softball in the park. The Dodgers were our baseball team and we were fiercely loyal and enthusiastic about our team. "Dem bums" were just like us, they were good, they were downhome and they were almost the tops. But for years the Yankees bested us in the World Series after we won the pennant of the National League. "Wait'll next year" was our cry, our mantra.

The first time I went to Ebbets Field to see the Dodgers play in person I was amazed at how beautiful the diamond looked: the grass was so green and bright, the bases gleamed white, and when the players came on the field I was in heaven, our heroes. We were very excited that Jackie Robinson, the first black player in the Major Leagues, was a Dodger, and a terrific player. After the game we went to the dugout and we children were allowed to run after the players who jogged slowly across the field so we could catch up to them and slip a self-addressed, folded postcard in one of their pockets. They mailed it back with their autograph. I caught up to Gil Hodges — he was very tall and I could just reach his front pocket with my arm extended. I remember receiving his signature but of course it's been lost in the shuffle of my life's belongings.

We had a song: "I'm Looking Over a Dodger Lineup" to the tune of "I'm Looking Over a Four Leaf Clover."

I'm looking over a Dodger Lineup that I overlooked before
Catching is Campy, on first is Gil
Second is Jackie and third is Bill
Shortstop is Pee Wee, left is Genie and center is the Duke
Right is Furill and on the hill is Preacher, the pride of the flock, oh what a pitcher Preacher, the pride of the flock.

Finally in 1955 the Brooklyn Dodgers beat the Yankees in the World Series. Our town went crazy. Rides on the trolleys and buses were free, free beer flowed in the bars. People were cheering and whooping it up all over the town. I was sixteen and I do admit I had not been following the games anymore. I was involved in my studies at school and in music. But I loved it; I knew how people felt and it was thrilling.

Two years later the veil was lifted. Baseball was Big Business now, and our beloved Dodgers were moved to Los Angeles. The owners wanted more fame, more fortune. We Brooklynites were bereft. We felt spurned, jilted, abandoned. The loyalty and love we gave our team was not wasted, we gave it freely and willingly. Now we directed our collective wrath at the owner, Walter O'Malley. The L.A. team carried the name "Dodgers," but the ethos of our team stayed with us in Brooklyn. It was the end of an era.

The 1950s

In the 1950s, I became a teenager, and my friends and I didn't play in the street like we did when we were younger. Well, with the exception of Ring-a-levio, a game of tag that originated on the streets of New York City. Ring-a-levio was still happening some nights, but mostly our point of destination was the ice-cream parlor. The candy store had been somewhat of a hangout the year before, but now we had crossed over 8th Avenue to Ehrich's Ice-Cream Parlor, a clean, well-lighted place for teenagers. We sat on stools at the counter or at tables in the back. We talked and gossiped until Mrs. Ehrich, who served us 10-cent sodas at the tables, made it clear as she wiped the table or stood nearby that we needed to order more drinks if we wanted to stay longer. Mr. Ehrich served us at the counter, and he was more lenient about time. I think he enjoyed having us schmoozing at his establishment. We never caused any trouble.

When we were ready, we went outside to sit on the nearby stoops or stand around in a motley circle to talk, sing, or plan parties and beach trips. Boys and girls sang lustily together old favorite songs about drinking and carousing. We also sang songs of the day, "Mule Train," "Sixteen Tons," and "Secret Love." The old songs that were passed down to us were parodies like this one to the tune of "The Caissons Go Rolling Along:"

Give a cheer, give a cheer for the boys (girls)
who drink the beer
In the cellars of old ______High
They are brave, they are bold for the whiskey they can hold

In the cellars of old _______High
For it's guzzle, guzzle, guzzle as it goes
right down your muzzle
Ring out your order loud and clear: MORE BEER

Another was to the tune of "The Quarter Master's Corps:"

For it's beer, beer, beer that makes you want to cheer,
in the corps,
For it's whiskey, whiskey, whiskey that makes you feel
so frisky, in the corps,
For it's mara, mara, juana that makes you
wanna, wanna, in the corps.

We had no experience with marijuana but if it was a good intoxicant, we approved!

We made up silly lyrics to well-known songs like "Jealousy." We sang:

Leprosy is crawling all over me.
There goes my eyeball into your highball...

Most everyone in my crowd of friends was Irish, and I loved when we sang this old chestnut:

"*T'was a cold winter evening the guests were all leaving*
O'Leary was closing the bar
When he turned and he said to the lady in red: "Get out
you can't stay anymore."
So she shed a sad tear in her bottle of beer when she
thought of the cold night ahead

When a gentleman dapper stepped out of the phone booth
and these are the words that he said:
Her mother never told her the things
a young girl should know
About the ways of college boys and how they
come and go, mostly go
Now age has taken her beauty and sin has left its great scar,
So remember your mothers and sisters, boys, and let her
sleep *under the bar."*

We sang this with great faux-emotional pathos.

We also sang these songs on the trolley car to Coney Island in the summer. Our go-to place at Coney Island was "Oceantide." It was a pool with a bar, jukebox and dance floor, on the boardwalk above one of the last bays of the ocean. We swam in the ocean, sunned on blankets on the sand, then paid our entrance to Oceantide where we swam some more and danced. The boys drank beer. There were places to buy sandwiches and hot dogs just outside Oceantide. "Mary's" was our favorite.

* * *

The Irish Catholic consciousness was strong in my group of friends, and here I was an outsider—even the enemy! My mother's father was born a Protestant, in Belfast, Ireland. I was orange Irish as opposed to their green. Daddy was also from a Protestant background. Happily for me his name was Rhyne, easily mispronounced as Ryan, a good green name, and that's how I "passed." Katy's surname was Kean, also possibly Irish, but like me, Katy was also a heretic Protestant. My four closest girlfriends knew the truth about me, but we never discussed this; our three Catholic girlfriends never mentioned it. All these dear Catholic friends were sure everyone wanted to be green Irish—I certainly did when I was a young teen. Later as my intellectual side developed, I was glad to not be so dogmatic and close-minded as my Catholic friends. I could accompany my girlfriends to their church service or wait in the back pew while they went to confession. They, however, could not come to my Presbyterian church; in those days that was a venial sin!

Sallie and Marty — 1955

My dearest friend Ann was a strong believer in Catholic superiority, but she loved me, her pet Protestant. Ann was my advocate in our group of friends, "the crowd." She made sure I was always included in parties, beach trips, and roller-skating outings. Because Ann lived upstairs from me, we went in and out of each other's homes freely. We often lent each other clothes, and one time she asked me if she could borrow a dress even before I wore it. Of course I said yes; I was so happy she liked it. To my dismay she returned it with sweat marks, and I could not show it to my mother who did the laundry. I said nothing to Ann or Mother. I buried the dress in the back of the packed closet and eventually forgot about it.

Ann was the assertive and bold conversationalist in our crowd. She noticed everything and had opinions on everything: what to do, what to wear, and how the Irish were the best of all ethnic groups. She referred to other groups pejoratively: wops, spics, kikes, and niggers.

This seemed to be the general thinking of all the green Irish that I knew. My parents did not allow us to use any pejorative terms. My brother Fred told me a story of watching a TV broadcast of a boxing match with Jackie, Ann's older brother. Jackie referred to the black contestant as the "n" word, and Fred referred to him as the guy in the white shorts or the other guy.

One evening Ann was holding forth, and she announced in her authoritative way that "The Jews are very clannish."

"Ye gods," I thought "more clannish than the Irish?"

I never said anything to oppose these prejudicial views. I behaved in my usual, quiet, and serene way. I loved my friends even though I internally rejected their biased attitude. I relished our scenes at the soda parlor, the parties, the dancing, the trips together on the trolley car to Coney Island, the singing, the cavorting in the park, and the occasional boyfriend.

One boyfriend I had was Marty. He was an older, red-haired, freckled-faced boy, who was AWOL from the army. This made him something of a hero to our crowd even though everyone was very patriotic. Marty was kind and gentle to me. He liked to have fun and laughed a lot. We danced together at parties, and one night we necked (closed-mouth kisses) in his car. I was in awe of his masculinity and his experience, but I had no idea of anything beyond kissing. He never attempted more. One night when he brought me home, he parked around the corner from my apartment house and planned to walk me home from there. It was late, maybe 11 p.m. As we got out of the car, who should we encounter, but my mother and father, who were out looking for me. Seeing us, Mother barked at Marty, "Do you know how old she is?" I was sixteen. He disappeared quietly, and I was marched home, and reprimanded for going in a car with an older boy. No one mentioned how polite and deferential he was. I was humiliated.

The next year when I was a senior at Bay Ridge High School, Ann did me a great favor when the prom was announced. It was to be at the Waldorf Astoria, a very swank hotel in Manhattan. The prom was to include a band for dancing, and I wanted to go. My first thought was to ask Raymond, a boy I had liked for years, to go with me. I called him on the phone and was surprised and embarrassed when he declined. I remember covering up my feelings by continuing to talk and making some

Top: Rita, Ann, Mary Jane
Bottom: Pat, Patsy, Sallie
— Coney Island 1955

Sallie and Katy — Coney Island Boardwalk 1955

kind of joke before I said good-bye. I told Ann, and she felt Raymond was a cad. Ann said she would make inquiries to get me a date.

Indeed she did. Hank was an older boy who was new to the crowd. He had seen action in Korea and was still shell-shocked, as we called PTSD in those days. Hank stayed away from firecrackers and fireworks on the Fourth of July. We all respected his fear. Ann found out that Hank was amenable to taking me to the prom and urged me to ask him. The next night I sat next to him at the counter at Ehrich's, and I popped the question. He agreed! What a relief. I was very lucky; not only was Hank tall and handsome, but also kind and thoughtful. He asked me to go on a few dates before the prom, so we could get to know each other. His sweet kisses were endearing.

We had a wonderful time at the prom. Ann Curry was a girl who organized our group of four couples, not to be confused with the Ann Curry who was my dear friend and upstairs neighbor. After the prom we went to the Village Barn and the Hawaiian Room, both nightclubs for more dancing and drinking mild alcoholic beverages. We ended up on the Staten Island Ferry, a tradition on prom night. We got home in the wee hours, which my parents expected. Mother and Daddy liked Hank; he was polite and unassuming, the kind of boy a parent would approve of for dates with their teenaged daughter.

This was 1956, the year we moved to the brownstone house on 4th Street. In the fall, I began Brooklyn College.

High School Graduation — 1956

The Mid-Fifties and Brooklyn College

As I began college in 1956, the marriages of my friends in the neighborhood also began. Ann was the first. We gave her a very lavish shower at a hall, many girlfriends and their mothers attended, and she received presents galore. Starting with a paper plate, we made her a hat from the ribbons and bows from all the wrappings, and she smiled coquettishly when we tied it on her head.

Ann's wedding was grandiose. Our bridesmaid's dresses were exquisite. Ann designed them with dark purple velvet scoop-necked bodices and lilac satin, wrap-around knee-length skirts—these were not the usual bridesmaid's dresses. These dresses were more sophisticated than the wide-skirted, puffy-sleeved, Cinderella-type. Years later,

Ann at her bridal shower — 1956

after several acid trips, purple became my favorite color, and I remembered this dress with appreciation for Ann's taste. Chic!

The church part of the wedding included a mass, and I refrained from taking communion. Ann did not object, and that showed me she had respect for my religion.

Katy Kean's marriage to Joe Maloney was a small affair. I was their witness at a registry office, and then she too embarked on her life as a wife and mother.

I was happy for my girlfriends, who were fulfilling their destiny, but I was very glad my path was different. I dove into my studies at Brooklyn College. I knew math was my best subject and would be my major, but I was interested in many things.

I fell in love with the writings of Thomas Paine, and on my own, I read all his works. *The Age of Reason* was thrilling to me; he debunked so much of the Bible's teaching. This was shocking and exciting—a new way of thinking! I knew right away that I was an agnostic. I grew up attending the Prospect Heights Presbyterian Church. I loved Jesus, but I questioned whether he was the "son of God," and whether the church that people created around his legacy was legitimate.

I was still attending church at this time because of the minister, Pastor Laughton. He was charismatic, intellectually astute, and widely traveled. His sermons were stimulating to me: he preached tolerance of all belief systems. He told stories about people all over the world who were kind to each other and forgiving of delinquency. I noted with disdain that the older ladies, who were so pious, often dozed off during Pastor Laughton's homilies. I confided in Pastor Laughton; I told him of my doubts about the Bible and the existence of God. Pastor Laughton listened and supported my critical thinking, and he never tried to convince me his views were right. He was not self-righteous in any way. I think he wanted me to follow my ideas, have life experiences, and draw my own conclusions.

Eventually, I had to leave the church. At age nineteen, I was a secular humanist, maybe even an atheist; I could no longer make a pretense of being a Christian. Those older pious ladies, who fell asleep during church, badgered my mother. "Where is Sallie? Why doesn't she come to church anymore?" they asked.

Finally Mother silenced them with the announcement: "Sallie is having doubts about the existence of God!" Mother believed in God, but she was sympathetic to me and my search for meaning. She also wanted the old biddies off her back!

* * *

The teacher of my first English class at Brooklyn College was a tall, thin man with sparkly eyes. He set us the task of describing him in a short essay, and then he would read some of these papers at random. I wrote:

"I am nervous and excited to meet my new English teacher. Will he be sympathetic to us freshmen? In walked a tall beanpole of a man with kind eyes and a brisk manner."

I watched him flip through the essays. I'm guessing "beanpole" caught his eye for it was my paper he read first. Thank goodness he did not know us by name, because I was embarrassed. He laughed good-naturedly at my description of him.

My freshman math class yielded more than mathematics—a new best friend. On the first day of class, I met Lynda and we are still friends to this day. Though we are different, we had an immediate rapport and linked up right away. Brooklyn College had a huge student population, and Lynda and I were shy. We felt the need for more social contacts, and our solution was to join a sorority. We met other young women that we liked and hosted interesting events. One event was a Halloween costume party. Lynda dressed as an Apache dancer with a tight skirt and a beret. I was Pocahontas with long braids of black wool and a fringed dress. We never met any boys we liked at those silly frat parties. My political consciousness was developing, and I realized that many sororities had racial requirements: you had to be white. I sent for the charter of Alpha Delta Pi, and I was horrified to see the racial requirement in writing. I immediately sent a letter of resignation, stating the reason. Lynda also left the group shortly afterwards.

Meanwhile, I loved my math classes but other subjects were compelling too. I took two Shakespeare classes. One was a survey of three plays: a Comedy, a Tragedy and a History. In the second class we read Hamlet line by line for the whole semester. The professor had a Freudian view of the play. He was of the opinion that "this too, too solid flesh" was really "sullied flesh." We looked at pictures of the original folios to see the word itself and why some scholars came to this conclusion. This attention to detail and delving into the original manuscripts was fascinating to me.

Lynda and I signed up for philosophy classes together. We had often had philosophical discussions, and

Daddy, Sallie, Mother — Brooklyn College Graduation 1960

Lynda, Sallie

we were exploring new ways of thinking. Somehow we got invited to parties that a New York University professor, Paul Edwards, gave at his Manhattan apartment. Professor Edwards wrote books on Bertrand Russell's ideas; Russell was one of our heroes. He was a mathematician as well as a free thinker. Professor Edwards gave us a letter of introduction to the great man, Bertrand Russell, when Lynda and I eventually went on our European trip. When we were in England we sent him the letter, but unfortunately he was not well, so we did not get to meet him.

I took a course in political science and my thinking here led me to Eugene Debs and Norman Thomas. Thomas founded the Socialist Party in America. Franklin Roosevelt had had talks with Norman Thomas when the New Deal was evolving. Brooklyn College had a chapter of the Debs Society. I attended their meetings and that led me to the Young People's Socialist League (YPSL) in Manhattan, headed by Michael Harrington who wrote "The Other America."

Michael Harrington was an inspiring speaker. Once he talked about socialism as being an orgiastic arrangement of society. I didn't understand orgasm or orgiastic, but I knew it meant ecstatic. I joined YPSL, which was the youth section of the Norman Thomas led Socialist Party. We had very stimulating lectures and discussions. One time we had a meeting and debate with the Young Americans for Freedom, a right wing group. It was a civilized debate and discussion. We also picketed Woolworths in solidarity with the sit-ins that were starting in the South.

I was dedicated to my math studies. I loved the abstract and advanced notions of calculus and vector analysis. No computer science for me, I was a pure mathematician! I decided to minor in physics, a science I found hard but akin to the mathematics I loved. My first physics teacher was a young and kind professor. I was the only female in the class, and he was sensitive to the fact that I was smart but shy. He allowed me to stand at my seat and outline the answer to the problem at hand. I dictated, and he wrote the solution on the blackboard. Everyone else wrote on the blackboard then faced the class to explain it. Later this teacher married a brilliant female physics major.

Rebel, Billy, Sallie — 1957

The second physics teacher was also young but thoroughly disconnected from his students. He came into the classroom late, his trench coat buttoned up, his hair in disarray, and his glasses atilt—the quintessential absent-minded professor. He knew his subject very well, but he had no interest in having a relationship with his students.

The best math teacher I had was Professor Griffin, a British woman who conveyed her love of mathematics, her quest for the most elegant solutions, and her concise and polished explanations. She would write on the blackboard as she elucidated the material and then turn to us and ask, "Are you with me?" She was always ready to answer questions. She demonstrated her ideal solutions with enthusiasm and charm. A tall woman, she was striking in her professional appearance.

Professor Griffin did me a great favor during my senior year at Brooklyn College. The Math Department was discussing which of the A students would be inducted into the math honors fraternity, Pi Mu Epsilon. When my name came up Professor Maria, a teacher I had for Advanced Calculus as a freshman, told the faculty group that I had gone to her and cried tears to get an A in her class. Untrue. I told Professor Griffin that was not me, and I remembered that Professor Maria had never learned my name. At the end of the semester when Professor Maria was handing out papers, she called my name and then looked all around the room; I was sitting right in front of her. Professor Griffin had violated the privacy of the faculty conversations by asking me about the incident with Professor Maria. Professor Griffin must have been satisfied by my explanation, because I did receive the honor.

Lynda and I were thrilled to graduate. We could now work for a year, live at home, and save money for a European trip. We would visit my relatives in Scotland, her family in Poland, and see the cultural high spots in France, England, Germany, and Austria. We both loved art and music. It was time to visit the great museums, hear the great orchestras play symphonies, and attend operas at the great opera houses.

After Brooklyn College: The World of Work

Bell Labs was the research division of AT&T. In 1960 their offices were in Manhattan near the Hudson River. I got a job there on the basis of my degree in math and graduating cum laude from Brooklyn College. The Bell Labs building was in an old public school building, very comfortable and familiar to me. My boss, Mr. Peek was a charming, affable man, short with a puckish face and a kindly manner. When I met him, I told him I didn't want to work on military projects. He excepted my caveat without question. He expected good work but left us alone to do it. His office was down the hall, and we didn't see much of him. I worked in a group with five or six men, who were very easy going. They welcomed me and helped me set up the experiments. As young and

Sallie at Bell Labs — 1960

inexperienced as I was, I felt no discomfort being the only woman in the group. They could tell that although I had little experience in circuitry, I learned quickly and had no trouble carrying out the projects and analyzing the results. I felt no gender discrimination and there were no comments about my being a woman.

My group did experiments on reed-relay switches. These were three inch oblong, glass tubes with two reeds inside that completed a circuit when they connected. The over-all objective here was to reduce a room full of large mechanical switches to a box of electronics: the Electronic Switching System, and I believe this is how the telephone company connects calls today. It was an interesting and challenging job for me. The reeds were coated with different substances and we tested the results in a telephone circuit.

Bell Labs had a workplace chorus, and I played the piano for their concerts. After I had been on the job for a few months, I heard about a job opening in another area of the building. I immediately told Lynda, my college buddy. She applied and secured that job. What a treat! We met on the subway in the morning and ate lunch together. There were some old-world bakeries in the neighborhood of Bell Labs where we bought delicious Jewish rye bread and other goodies.

Later that winter, a new young man joined my group. Frank was a handsome, sweet man who sat next to me. I thought he would be a perfect match for Lynda. She came to see me at an arranged time, and I introduced them. I saw Frank's face light up as he leaned back in his chair to look at Lynda. My matchmaking instincts were satisfied. Lynda and Frank were together for many years.

Lynda and I hatched a plan to go together on a trip to Europe after working for a year, living at home, and saving money. We would visit my mother's family in Scotland, see Paris and Rome, and then visit Lynda's relatives in Poland. We procured the necessary visas, and passports in the spring.

I was still involved with the Young People's Socialist League (YPSL.) Everyone was affected by the Cold War saber rattling of our government and the USSR. This was an era of air-raid drills. A drill was planned in the late spring for us at Bell Labs. We were instructed to follow the directions of the Air-Raid Wardens, leave our desks, and file out of the building. I planned to protest by not following directions and staying put at my desk. Lynda came from her office and Frank joined us in our demonstration against air-raid drills. We sat in my office and talked together as everyone else left. People were very surprised, even shocked by our disobedience. The next day Mr. Peek called me into his office. "Are you a Quaker?" he queried me, "I can't believe you are a communist." I wouldn't say anything about my affiliations, just that I didn't think air-raid drills were helpful in preventing war. On the contrary, they were preparing people for war. The following day I received in my inbox, an application for Top Secret Clearance. Mr. Peek was following orders from his superiors to find out all about me. I took the application to his office and said, "I won't be needing this. I am going on a trip and resigning my job." I parted company with all on good terms.

Lynda and I bustled around getting things we thought we would need: clothes for warm and cold weather, toiletries, even toilet paper, because we had heard it was scarce in some countries. We bought humungous, twenty-nine inch suitcases. My dad had an idea: attach wheels to the bottom of these huge, awkward suitcases, so we could roll them around easily. He actually used old skate wheels that made a skittery sound. Dear Dad, he always wanted to win a lot of money. He played the horses when he was young. Later he would enter contests in newspapers. If only he had patented his invention!

Lynda and I booked passage on one of the Cunard ocean liners, the smallest one, but it was very large to us. We were in second class, and we met some other young women that we liked and had fun with. Then we met some guys who worked on the ship's crew and they invited us to parties in their quarters. We had to walk through first class to get to the crew quarters for the rowdy parties. The crew guys were very respectful to us despite the fact that we were all drinking beer or wine and carousing noisily.

We landed in Cork, Ireland. The landscape was typically and beautifully green and glowing. We kissed the blarney stone and went to Dublin in search of culture. We saw a play and found bed and breakfast places. With clean and old-fashioned décor, these places were charming and the folks served us thick bread and homemade jam.

After a few days we took a boat to Scotland. I was surprised by my first glimpse of Glasgow; it was a port with large ships and cranes and tough looking men lining the waterfront. We took public transportation to my Aunt Peggy's house. It was a small place in a residential area with tree-lined streets and grassy yards. Aunt Nan lived around the corner in her modest apartment. Neither home had a refrigerator. Each had a screened-in recess in a kitchen wall that jutted outside where eggs, milk and butter were kept. I had three boy cousins, Billy, Bobby and Hugh, very friendly and good-natured children. My uncle spoke with such a thick burr we had trouble understanding him. The weather was good, two weeks of summertime with little rain and lots of sun.

We moved on to London, visiting the Tate Gallery, the Tower of London, and other tourist stops. Our suitcases were cumbersome even with wheels, and we realized that we didn't need to cart so much stuff around. In Paris we stored these behemoths at the American express and bought smaller bags to carry on the trains. With our Eurail passes, we chugged around France and Italy, talking to friendly people who spoke English.

The effects of the War were still glaringly evident in Berlin: bombed out buildings and streets with shells of homes. We took a train through East Germany and Czechoslovakia on the way to Poland. The colorful and prosperous look of Western Europe changed to gray and gloomy on this part of the journey. Large signs in bold red letters proclaimed the glorious communist states in contrast to the drab and dreary sights outside the train windows. When officials came on board the train at borders, I got nervous. I had a bunch of democratic socialist reading material in my luggage. I planned to give away these tracts in Poland. Luckily no one searched our suitcases. We were innocent in so many ways, and we did not look suspicious to the officious officials who tramped through the cars looking hard at people

We stopped in Krakow, Poland to see the wooden church altar in the street with large cobblestones. It was hot and cold drinks were not available since there was no refrigeration in Krakow in 1961. People were very friendly and Lynda spoke Polish. In Warsaw, we stayed with Lynda's relatives. They had little material goods compared to what we had in America, but they shared everything they had with us. Lynda's aunts cooked us delicious meals and took us to see the sights. The Old City in Warsaw was kept as it had been before the War. We saw a young man there who looked bohemian; he was painting on a canvas outdoors. We went to a college and asked to speak to some students about their lives. The students we were directed to were party-line communists, and I decided against handing out my seditious reading material.

We went to visit Chopin's birthplace on a beautiful autumn day. The sun shone brightly on the orange and red deciduous tree leaves. It was there I had the realization that all my life, I thought the sun did not shine behind the "iron curtain." That woke me up to the power of words: the power of suggestion on a young mind. Maybe I became more skeptical and more discriminating in forming my beliefs after that. It was an illuminating moment.

Departure for Europe — 1961

Lynda — Warsaw 1961

Lynda — Piazza San Marco, Venice 1961

Lynda, Aunt Peggy, Sallie — Glasgow 1961

Climate Change

After our time in Poland, Lynda and I trucked around and ended up in Vienna. Lynda revealed that she was homesick; she missed her boyfriend Frank, and she wanted to go home to New York City. I was surprised but willing to say goodbye for the moment, because I felt no such pull to go home. I was determined to stay away as long as I could on my dwindling finances. I inherited frugality from my mother, and I was sure I could eke out a few more months.

I rented a room in a house in Vienna. Mrs. Suhanek was very generous; she would knock on my door and offer me delicious home-cooked meals, not included in the rent. I must have looked like I needed fattening up. Lunch for me was at the student mensa, the local college cafeteria where I could eat a hearty meal for the equivalent of twenty-two cents. Given the cold weather, even after I ate every bit off my own plate, I would lust after the leftovers on the students' plates. I bought a loaf of Dawa Brot from a bakery every few days: dark pumpernickel, warm from the oven. I would eat almost the whole loaf in one sitting.

I was lonely without Lynda, but *mirabile visu* I met Margaret, an American girl, in my German class who, like me, was interested in the arts. We went to the Staats Oper, Vienna's famous opera house, for four schillings and stood in the back swooning over operas by Verdi, Puccini and Mozart. Often couples would leave at intermission and give us their tickets. Then we sat in the orchestra section and sopped up the gorgeous sounds in comfort.

To keep warm during that snowy, freezing winter of 1961, we would visit the Art Museum for the stupendous collections of Titian, Rembrandt, Caravaggio, among others. The library was another haven. Unfortunately, the social climate was as chilly as the weather. We tried to meet some young people, who we would see in coffee houses and around town but without success. We wondered if we, as Americans, were getting the cold shoulder because of the War: i.e., we won, they lost. It had been only sixteen years since that terrible conflict ended. Maybe these young Viennese were just reserved in their temperament, and they were not interested in meeting foreigners. "Well," we reasoned, "no need to stay here any longer. Let's head out to warmer climes and perhaps more congenial company."

Spain seemed a likely choice. So we packed our bags and set off to hitchhike to our destination.

Margaret and I had good luck finding a ride and soon found ourselves in the Austrian countryside—so charming in the snow. Each village had church steeples rising above the snow-whiteness into the blue skies. The people we met were friendly and generous with rides, and very soon we were in Italy where the air was warmer and the men strutted around like cocks in a barnyard, hoping we would look at them. We did!

In France the youth hostels were coed; there were no separate bedrooms for male and female. Margaret had slept with her boyfriend, but neither one of us was interested in sleeping with strangers, which was an option.

One day, I hopped in the front seat, and Margaret hopped in the back seat of a low-slung sports car with a masher. He tried to impress us by driving very fast along the curvy roads and at a one point draped his arm around me. Margaret whapped him with her umbrella from the back seat. He was chastened.

Spain was even warmer than Italy. The Spanish people opened up to us: we were invited to dinner, to see the sights, and to walk on the Ramblas in Barcelona. My high school Spanish served me well and being immersed allowed my fluency to develop.

With the deep blue Mediterranean on one side of the road, and the green hillside with colorful wild flowers on the other side, hitchhiking was a delight on the Costa del Sol. Once, we were in a car behind a truck laden with bright, succulent Valencia oranges. The truck hit a bump and oranges bounced out, rolling on the road. Our driver stopped, and we all gathered the sweet, golden fruit to share. This was our Shangrila, but it wasn't without a dark side. We went to a bullfight and were horrified. I got physically sick when the picadors were stabbing the bull with their spears. We left, saddened by the cruelty.

Margaret and I were very compatible. We had similar feelings and opinions. She was a year younger than me, but since she had already been intimate with a man, I thought of her as more experienced, more worldly. We didn't discuss intimacy, however, we kept to art, music, and other cultural aspects of life, languages, and customs different from our own. The world was unfolding before our eyes and we were thrilled.

In Granada, we relished the Alhambra with its exquisite Moorish architecture and art. I wandered over to the hillside opposite the grand building where Spanish gypsies lived. I met a young boy, about ten or twelve years old who wanted to show me his home, a cave carved into the hillside. There was a white wooden fence in front where his mother greeted and invited me into their clean and colorful place. I had figured out that in this region, Andalucia, the people elided the ess in their language. "Hasta la vista" was "ha ta la vi ta." The mother and I talked, and she showed me the lovely handmade cooking utensils and decorative pieces hanging from the ceiling. The pieces of polished copper gleamed and were, of course, for sale. She was very gracious when I admired her work, but I did not buy anything. Her son was ready to go out again and show me a special church on the back of the hill. It was indeed special. It was a Catholic church with a six-pointed Star of David as its religious symbol.

Margaret and I were entranced with our experiences in Spain and kept moving south. We met an English boy, about our age with similar travel intentions, so the three of us made our way to Algeciras. Here was the promise of even greater adventure: a ferry ride across the Straits of Gibraltar would bring us to Tangier, Morocco—only one dollar to be transported to another continent. Who could resist? We embarked.

MOROCCO

Morocco 1962

For Margaret and me, a new level of excitement was coming to our travels. We were not in Europe anymore—we were in North Africa! We had taken the ferry from Algeciras to Tangier, and we were met at the dock by young Arab boys. They were multilingual and they tagged us as Americans. These youngsters offered to take us to the Casbah, the Medina, the old Arab quarter of the city, as opposed to the European section with its tall buildings and town houses.

We registered at the youth hostel a few feet away from the dock and off we went with our guides. The streets of the Casbah were unpaved and labyrinthine. Donkeys plodded along laden or unladen with their people in tow. Women were clothed in purdah, a long tailored dress with a headpiece that only allowed eyes to show. It was fascinating. Our guides took us to a tourist shop with beautiful handcrafted items: rugs, wall hangings, teapots, and ceramic dinnerware. We were not buying, but the vendors served us mint tea, the quotidian drink of the people. Made with a heap of fresh mint leaves, the tea was very sweet with sugar. They served the tea in a teapot shaped like a peaked cap.

We stayed many days wandering through the Medina, observing the people and their customs. The bread bakers carried their fresh, round loaves on their heads to the market place. The Berber farmers, who lived outside the city limits of Tangier, brought their produce and goat cheese on palm leaves. They would come barefoot, wearing white robes that wrapped around their bodies and carried their wares and their babies. The Berbers are the indigenous people of Morocco. In the North, they are light-skinned. Many had freckles and blue eyes like their ancestors from Northern Europe.

We wanted to see more of this exotic land, so we hitchhiked south along the coast to Rabat, the capital of Morocco. We were not afraid to ride with strangers—always men in this country—women did not drive in the 1960s. Our sense of security, our belief in the goodness of people seems naïve today, but it was compelling in those days, so on we went. John, the English boy we had met in Spain left us somewhere along the way, but Margaret and I were undeterred in our pursuit of adventure.

We found ourselves in Ouarzazate, inland, close to the Sahara Desert. Our driver was the chief of police of the area, and he was generous to us. He took us to his friend's house for dinner, and what a sumptuous feast it was. We sat on the floor around a low round table. The host brought around a basin of water and towels for hand washing. Water was poured from a peaked cap teapot into the basin for each person. We ate delicious couscous with meat and vegetables without utensils. We scooped up portions of the brew with pieces of bread. Margaret and I, along with the men were the only ones at the table; we never saw the women who prepared the food. After dinner the police chief threw each of us a cellophane wrapped package: nightgowns. We got it. They wanted to sleep with us.

"Monsieur, vous avez fait un faux pas!" Margaret said, emphatically in her perfect French.

To our great relief we were taken to another place to spend the night alone.

The next day the chief recommended a tourist hotel

in the next town to the south, Zagora. His friends ran the hotel and would give us a good deal. Never daunted, off we went. The town was very close to the Sahara and rather desolate looking: red, scrabbly sand, a few small adobe homes, tent homes, and a market that only had dates for sale: piles of various varieties of dates, but nothing else. The hotel was large and empty; we were the only guests. The managers were naturally thrilled to have us and suggested an outing for the next day: they would take us to a lovely town next to a river. We agreed and left to explore Zagora on our own.

We were surprised to see a German boy of our age walking around town. We approached and talked to him. His name was Hans, he spoke English, and he joined us in our explorations. We then met three young Arab boys about our age who were friendly and spoke French. They invited us to lunch and during the conversation we mentioned the trip planned for the next day with the men at the hotel. These three Arabs were shocked, "That town is on the Algerian border and the white slave market does business there. Don't go!"

We leapt up and ran like the wind to the hotel to retrieve our belongings. The managers were perplexed as we raced in and out, calling out "Goodbye!" We were not taking any chances here. We dashed back to our rescuers, where we set up with Hans in a room in their tent house.

That evening our hosts prepared dinner for us. As an appetizer we were offered almonds with sprinkled green flakes. Delicious, but as we nibbled I detected a change in my perception. I felt like I was observing myself from outside myself. I started to describe this feeling to Margaret in English, which our hosts did not understand. “Yes,” she said, “go on, I feel strange too.” It wasn’t long before we realized that we were eating hashish, and our defenders were probably expecting that we would become uninhibited; maybe we would dance wildly to the music that was playing, maybe invite them to our bed. Neither one of us wanted this, so we retreated to our room and took Hans with us. We were so nervous about the situation that we insisted Hans sit up all night with his hunting knife on the table.

It’s amazing how many times we put ourselves in possible dangerous situations and how the men involved behaved like gentlemen, with genuine humanity. They accepted our refusal to go along with their desires without hostility or resentment.

Our young Arab friends did not bother us that night and in the morning greeted us with no questions. They told us of a bus that left at three in the morning to go to a desert oasis, Muhammad. We signed up and left early the next day. There was no road to this oasis and the driver navigated by the stars. We stopped at small encampments of people along the way. Perhaps they were nomads. The people were destitute; the children had suppurating eyes surrounded by flies. They looked to us for help, for coins, or maybe just for sympathy. I hoped the bus brought them supplies.

Hours later we reached the Sahara. Huge sand dunes were everywhere; the wind blew the sand hither and yon. The atmosphere was bleak. The bus parked at the only “store” in the area, which had little to offer. It was a ramshackle wooden building that looked out of place in this sandy space. On the bus we had made friends with a Jewish man who spoke many languages including the Berber language of this region. We had noticed that as we went further south in Morocco the Berber people were darker skinned with African features. The people here were the Tuareg,"The Blue People," so named, because they wore dark blue robes that had been dyed with a local plant. The women wore silver jewelry, which was their money, and it stood out beautifully against their dark skin and robes.

These people were Islamic, but they combined religion with their native customs and beliefs. Our friend from the bus said he would take us to visit a family he knew. We followed him down a road away from the others to see this family at their home. An older woman greeted us at the door. She smiled broadly when she saw Margaret and me. Our friend explained that this woman, the matriarch, thought we were nurses. Apparently, the only other white people she had seen were nurses, who gave the family vaccinations. She invited us in. Now our friend became nervous. Only women and girls stayed at home, and if the men came home unexpectedly from the fields and found him there, he explained, they would use those curved knives they wore around their necks on him!

We stayed long enough to have goat's milk and dates. We sat on the floor on mats around a low table. The young girls were amazed at our presence. They were shy and pulled their shawls over their faces, but we saw their smiles. As we were leaving, the matriarch suggested that Margaret stay with them. Margaret had long, blonde hair and that was considered a prize. Margaret's refusal was accepted graciously; the old woman grinned a wide smile that showed her missing teeth. We departed gratefully, thanking her for her hospitality.

Continuing the Journey

Margaret and I were living in the present moment. We had so many unusual experiences, one after another. We hardly talked about any one event for another was upon us, and that's where we were focused. I didn't keep a journal, but the occurrences were indelibly impressed on my consciousness. Later I thought about these happenings with amazement. There was danger lurking on the edges of our experiences, but we gave that no credibility; we never let that possibility grow large. We believed deeply in our ability to shape our lives, to live our lives without harm to ourselves. We trusted the universe.

We had seen some of the western and southern areas of Morocco; now we were headed back to Spain via eastern Morocco. We traveled, hitchhiking north through the Atlas Mountains, thrilled by the beauty of the landscape: green wooded forests on steep mountains. We were now in a temperate zone where it was cold in winter and snow capped the high mountains. There were ski resorts here.

We passed through Fez, an ancient city of intellectual and spiritual significance. Scholars of all faiths came to Fez to study at the university that was founded in the tenth century. The maze of unpaved streets that was the Casbah in Fez was even narrower and more archaic than Tangier. There was a feeling of ancient time or timelessness, and at the same time the many tourist shops confirmed it was the twentieth century.

Back in Tangier, we retraced our steps across the Straits of Gibraltar to Algiceras and took a train to Madrid. Margaret was getting in touch with her mother and arranging to meet her in Germany. We said goodbye, hoping to meet again another time. Sadly, we never did. I was about to return to Tangier with plans to stay for a while and then return to New York on the Yugolinea, a Yugoslavian freighter that took on some passengers and charged a hundred dollars for the trip to New York. Fate had other plans.

I was not in a hurry, so I looked on bulletin boards at the Youth Hostel and the American Express office in Madrid for a hitchhiking partner. I found "Red," a tall red-haired Canadian boy, who was friendly and headed in my direction. We had good luck hitching and then it was nighttime. There was no hostel in the town, and he suggested taking one room in a hotel. "We'll save money and you will be perfectly safe with me," he assured me. I was reluctant but went along. He registered us as a married couple and requested two beds. Tucked up separately we chatted into the night. Suddenly, he jumped up and came to sit on my bed. "Oh you're so sweet," he cooed.

"Yes, but you said I'd be safe," I replied, pulling up the covers, my virgin state threatened. Red was a gentleman and didn't press his case. We slept chastely and continued our journey in the morning.

I had sent Margaret a postcard describing Red as a "cool cat," who I met and would go hitching with to Tangier. Later when my mother had not heard from me for several weeks, she somehow got in touch with Margaret, and my dear friend sent that postcard to my mother! This caused my parents great consternation, and they were ready to call Interpol. More about this later.

We arrived in Tangier on a bright and sunny day, once more entering the Arab world I thought I knew something about. Red moved on, and I signed into the Youth Hostel near the dock on the edge of the Medina. The hostel "father" was Mohammed. He was friendly, even protective in his manner. "Let me get those things for you, some people are dangerous for young girls," he offered. Mohammed would get your money changed on the black market or provide you with marijuana or other drugs if you so desired.

The next day Mohammed invited me to meet an American boy he knew. I was ready for more adventure, and agreed. Ron was tall and lanky, a lock of light brown hair falling over his eyes made him look boyish and attractive to me. We had lunch in a café and he offered me a ride on his Vespa scooter. "Sure," I replied. I felt comfortable with him. We whizzed around the Casbah and the European section of town. It was exhilarating and exciting to hold onto his manly body and feel his strength. Tinglings of new feelings coursed through me.

"I know people here in the Medina," he said, "Americans, Canadians, Europeans. Beat poets live here also." I was intrigued. Here was a world I had read about but never been a part of. Ron's friends were mostly male. I only met one girl, Jean, who wasn't around very much. People were coming and going all the time, traveling south to Marrakesh or north to Europe, but Ron's best friend, Gordon was a mainstay. Ron and Gordon were together most days.

People lived together in rented places in the Medina, adobe houses with shared bathrooms and no kitchens. Many had no running water, so they collected their water from a common well near the house. We all spoke Spanish to our Arab friends, who were all men. The women were very sheltered. They wore purdah, a long tailored robe with a headpiece that revealed only their eyes. Later I met some Arab girls who wore modern dress to their jobs in the European section and purdah at home in the Medina.

Day by day I was drawn into Ron's circle. I joined them in smoking "keef," a mixture of marijuana and uncured tobacco leaf. Our Arab friends were meticulous in chopping the ingredients to a certain thickness and then mixing them together in a particular ratio. They warned us against smoking marijuana straight. *"Se vuelve loco!"* We said nothing but when they were not around we rolled a joint and smoked it.

One hardly needed marijuana to be high in Tangier in 1962. Just walking around the narrow winding streets of the Casbah with its teeming crowds of people dressed in robes, and their donkeys and goats ambling along with bells on their leashes, was enough to give me the impression that I was on another planet, a long way from New York City or the European cities I had visited. The smells of Arab spices: cumin, turmeric, and others piled high in the marketplace; all this, the guttural sound of the Arabic language, the exotic music playing on unfamiliar instruments in who-knows-what time signature, was other-worldly to me.

We went to the Zoco Chico and the Zoco Grande, two outdoor plazas in the Medina with cafés to drink mint tea and watch people. We saw Gregory Corso and Ted Joans, two well-known Beat poets. William Burroughs had just left, we heard. Ron and Gordon wrote prose and poetry and looked to these published authors for inspiration. We were discreet and never approached these luminaries, even when we attended a party at a beautiful Medina home where the celebrities hobnobbed.

I tabled my plans to return home, becoming more and more fascinated by this bohemian scene and falling in love with Ron. I could tell Gordon wanted to be closer to me—we were often all three together—but I chose Ron.

After I moved to an apartment in the European section, Ron convinced me to move back to the Medina and together we rented a room in a hotel. He bought a straw mattress and some kitchen utensils and we moved in. Then we went out to dinner. When we returned I wasn't sure if this was my room or our room. I half expected him to leave but we sat on the bed together and he started to make love to me. I was amazed. I really didn't think I was sexually attractive, especially to someone as tall and good-looking as Ron. He made me feel otherwise. I let myself follow his lead. He was a very gentle lover. He knew he was initiating me as he peeled away my clothes and some of my deeply ingrained inhibitions. I had just turned 23.

Deflowered

The next morning I awoke in a daze. I was confused by this new experience. I had been so sexually repressed; I had never touched my vagina except for the quick wipe of a washrag or toilet paper. Once when I was sixteen, I was sitting on the lap of a boyfriend, we were kissing, sweet closed-mouth kisses. He asked me, "Do I excite you?" I had no idea what he meant and said honestly, "No."

Ron knew he had to protect me from pregnancy and the next day he took me to a French woman doctor who examined me and fitted me for a diaphragm. This sensation of being opened in that genital way was like a breakthrough that I didn't understand. A boundary had been crossed. I wasn't in control of my body, and for reasons I didn't understand that led me to the odd feeling that I was my mother. If I was my mother then I was having sex with my father. This was traumatizing. I lived in a hallucinatory, catatonic state, unable to speak for about two weeks.

Ron carried on being my lover and my best friend. I adored him for that. I was hemmed into myself by a psychological cage and could not say what was happening to me. I was not hysterical but rather impassive and detached. Ron acted as if nothing was amiss. He and Gordon talked endlessly about *The Naked Lunc*h, William Burroughs' novel and other Beat classics. They cut up their own writings and pasted them back together in random ways as per Burroughs. Was this a statement about reality? About art reflecting reality? About the randomness of the universe? What was reality anyway? Did anything make real sense? These questions were bantered about constantly.

At the same time our Arab friends, all men, started teaching me how to cook in their style. We used a ceramic bowl on the floor with small pieces of coal and a short stub of a candle to cook a stew in one pot. The stew was vegetables and beef, flavored with pungent spices.

Slowly my voice returned and I felt more comfortable. Things were returning to normal for me.

All our Arab friends who came to our place were men. We had no contact with Arab women. They were totally sheltered from meeting strangers. I did see female vendors at the marketplace, but they were Berber women from the countryside. Later I would meet some young Arab women and get a glimpse into their lives.

Our Arab friends also taught me how to bargain in the marketplace. They informed me of the real prices of food and goods we needed and insisted that I haggle with the sellers.

"Se hace asi!" (This is how it is!) they persisted. My Spanish improved greatly in this process as I got into it, and the highest compliment I received after agreeing on a price with a vendor was his query: *"Tu eres espanola?"* (Are you Spanish?)

I busied myself with household duties, and one day I wanted to make an American style casserole for dinner. We had no oven but I had an idea. I made the casserole in a Pyrex dish I bought at the market and took it to the bread bakers. Their ovens were ancient stone recessed affairs with the fire deep in the chamber. They used a wide, wooden paddle to put the round, flat loaves in and out of the oven. They agreed to bake my dish for a few cents after exclaiming how odd it was. We waited outside and talked while the dish cooked.

"*Porque estas aqui?*" (Why are you here?) "*Queremos ir a America.*" (We want to go to America.) "*Su país estan rica pero somos pobres.*" (Your country is rich, we are poor.")

I replied, "*Estoy interesada en otras culturas. Quiero ver como otro gente vive.*"

(I am interested in other cultures. I want to see how others live.) They were amazed at this point of view. They seemed to think the object of life was to be rich.

Ron and Gordon approved of my culinary experiments; I was happy playing a female role, but mostly they were busy with their affairs: writing, talking, getting high and playing music with our Arab friends. Ron bought himself ceramic drums and tried to learn the complicated rhythms and timing of Arab music. There were ongoing discussions of the size of the drums, the skin material that covered them as well as the actual playing. I made no effort to count the time or understand the rhythms intellectually. I just enjoyed the exotic flavor of the music I heard day and night in the city and at home at these jam sessions.

We had a friend named Mohammed (so many Arab men had this name) who visited us. He was a dancer in a restaurant/nightclub where he balanced a tray with a tea service on his head while dancing. Mohammed never danced at our place, but he gave me a picture postcard, which I still have showing him performing this feat. He played instruments at the jam sessions.

One evening Ron and I went at his invitation to Mohammed's home for dinner. We sat in a small room curtained off from the rest of the house. His wife handed in delicious dishes for us, but she didn't eat with us; in

Mohammed dancing — Morocco 1962

fact we never saw her. Mohammed took the food at the curtain and then sat down with us to eat. After the meal his wife passed in the baby for us to admire and dandle on our laps. Evidently the baby was worthy of to be with us, but she, the mother, was not. Then she passed in tea for us. I was so upset by this situation that I spilled the hot tea in my lap.

Ron and I never discussed the oppressive conditions under which the Arab women lived. We were visitors in this country, and we observed everything and criticized nothing. I was affected seeing the low status Mohammed's wife accepted as her fate, but philosophically I knew I could do nothing to change that.

Deeper 1962

In Tangier there was a feeling of timelessness; we didn't read newspapers or listen to the radio. Often we didn't know what day of the week it was. But we knew when it was Friday, the Arab Holy Day, because many shops were closed. We knew when it was Sunday for the American Express office was closed then. We went to that office to get our mail and to hear some news of the world outside the Casbah.

Smoking keef every day and adjusting to a new life of love and sex with Ron in this exotic place was enough to make me forget my other life, i.e., my relationship and duties to my parents. I wrote letters to them about the landscape, the food and the different culture of Tangier, never anything about what was really happening to me. That would have disturbed them and upset them, so I left that out. I must have let weeks go by without writing, and one day I went to the American Express and picked up a telegram from my mother. It read: "Come home at once we are about to call Interpol." This is an international police force that locates people everywhere in the world. My Aunt Janet had sent Mother and Daddy a newspaper clipping on the white slave market in Morocco. And Margaret had sent the postcard about my meeting a "cool cat" to hitchhike with. My parents were distraught. I imagined Interpol going from house to house in the Medina looking for me. I rushed to the Telephonia, an office where you could call anywhere in the world. Fortunately I reached my mother.

"Mother I'm so happy to talk to you, I'm fine. The mail is slow in this medieval country, and I'm caught up in my explorations of this intriguing city! I have some American and Canadian friends now and we keep busy traveling and savoring the sights." Thankfully, I allayed her fears.

There were three young Arab women working at the Telephonia who helped me with my call. They were very friendly and wore Western dress, no veil. I felt comfortable with them and broached the subject of clothes. We spoke in Spanish. "You wear European dress," I started, "why not the purdah that I see other Arab women wearing?"

"We are required to dress this way for our jobs here," said Fatima, the most outgoing of the three. "We wear purdah at home and on the weekends, we think it's beautiful." Fatima invited me to her home for tea on the weekend. "I'd like to show you where we live and how we look there."

"Thank you, I'd love to come," I replied. I was grateful for this invitation.

We met at Fatima's home, and they all wore purdah dresses in subdued colors. Fatima's home was simple and neat with colorful Arab wall hangings. She lived with her mother, father, and siblings, but I did not see or meet them. I thought of these young women as in transition, between two worlds, the traditional and the modern European style.

The Arab-Jewish tension was prominent in Morocco. Many people spoke about Jews being deported. Our friend Dan, an American Jew, was beset by Arab guys who harassed him and made his life in the Casbah difficult. Paradoxically our Arab men friends revered "La Judia," an elderly Jewish crone, who was said to be clairvoyant and have extra-normal powers: a shaman. One day these friends took Ron and me to see her. She was a small, thin, wizened woman who sat on a mat in an old back-street abode. People gathered around her at a respectful distance and asked her questions. Later one of our friends said, *"Hay muchas cosas en todo el mundo."*

This resonated with me very deeply. I'm sure this man had never read "Hamlet" who said, "There are more things in heaven and earth, Horatio, than are dreamt of in your philosophy."

* * *

At the hotel where we lived we saw couples having sex standing up in the courtyard. We became aware of an English-speaking man upstairs who entertained Arab boys each day. "This place is a brothel!" Ron exclaimed one day, "Let's move." We had lived in this place for about a month. Now we wanted to live with ordinary family people, so we located an adobe house deeper in the Medina that we rented with two other male friends, one Arab, one American. We had separate rooms, but we lived communally and shared the bathroom. That room had no shower or tub, only a strange toilet with no seat. You squatted over a hole in the floor, but there was some flush mechanism.

There were two places to have a bath or a shower. The *hamman* was a hot, steamy sauna place with baths and showers. There was a separate women's section. At another smaller place, men and women could shower in a European shower stall with a closed door. One day I went there for a shower and a man in the stall next to me shimmied up the wall between us to peep at me. I yelled out, *"Un hombre sobre la pared!"* (A man on top of the wall!) He got down, and when I came out clean and dressed he tried to pick me up.

"Tu eres bonita," he cooed. I refused to look at him and stormed out, never to return.

One morning I woke up nauseous and knew immediately I was pregnant. Ron and I had been faithful in the use of the diaphragm; it must have happened that first night. I was distressed; this was not what I wanted. Neither Ron nor I was prepared to commit to raising a child. As usual Ron came to the rescue. He found an English doctor, who would do an abortion in his office high atop a hill in the European section.

This man was kind and understanding. After examining me, he asked me why I wanted to terminate the pregnancy. "We're not married," I answered. "I'm not ready to raise a child, especially here in this environment so far from my home."

"Fine," he said and we made an appointment. The doctor was experienced in these matters and had a comfortable bed in a side room where I woke up to see Ron smiling at me. "Feel okay, baby?" he queried.

"Yes, just groggy," I replied.

"I'll take good care of her," Ron assured the doctor. I was young and healthy and soon recovered. I had no regrets.

My parents were satisfied with the letters I wrote home describing the beautiful views of the Mediterranean Sea, the gorgeous beaches, the ethnic dress and customs of the Arabs and the Berbers in Tangier. My mother saved these letters for me, which I appreciated very much. Mother and Daddy relaxed, and I carried on with my illicit affair and bohemian existence with no thought as to where this might lead.

Deeper in Trouble 1962

Our circle of friends was at last finished with William Burroughs and his text *The Naked Lunch*. Someone introduced a completely different book: *The I Ching or Book of Changes.* We were open, and we were pursuing truth in its many forms. I who had majored in math and science in college, who had given up belief in God for lack of evidence, was fascinated by a book of Chinese wisdom incorporating Taoism and Confucianism. This book purported to explain the personal and larger natural universe by chance. You could use yarrow stalks (the stems of the yarrow flower), which we didn't have, or coins that we did have to build a hexagram of six lines, some straight, some broken. Yang lines were straight, Yin lines broken. Your hexagram had Chinese and English names; sixty-four readings elaborated and explained the meaning of the hexagram, general information, and specific meanings for certain lines. Asking a question would bring up readings such as "The Creative," "The Receptive," "Peace," or "Standstill." We felt the book was a powerful guide to understanding ourselves and the mysterious world we lived in.

Ron was learning to use the I Ching, like the rest of us, but otherwise, he was the guru in our circle. He was very knowledgeable; he had read the relevant books and had opinions on them. He knew jazz and jazz artists, and he had been in the army. Later, I learned he had used heroin and had been in jail in California. He was very tall, six foot four and a half, and his soft personality endeared him to all. Gordon said, "Ron is God."

We were high every day smoking keef and joints of

straight marijuana. Our Arab friends brought us the pot, which we purchased from them. But one day Ron got the idea to go to the source—Mount Ketama—where the stuff was grown. We hitched a ride in the back of a pick-up truck and off we went. It was maybe an hour's drive bumping along in the back of that beat-up, old truck till we came to the area. The hills glowed chartreuse with flourishing marijuana plants. We stopped at an outpost that had wooden barns bulging with supplies. Ron bargained with the Arab sellers and bought a kilo (about two pounds). He hid his stash under a raincoat he draped over his arm when we returned to Tangier.

Unfortunately a local Arab dealer, Benny, saw Ron and ripped away the coat to expose the contraband. Everyone smoked keef but officially it was illegal. Benny thought Ron was dealing pot to the tourists, Benny's purview, so he informed the police and Ron was busted. They put him in jail while I was at the market, unable to protest. Gordon and I pondered the situation and tried to come up with a plan. We decided that I would claim to be Ron's wife and demand to see him. We would not inform the American Embassy since those diplomats would not support our right to buy and smoke marijuana, even in Tangier.

So I applied to the city bureaucracy, in the European section of town, as Ron's wife and said he was wrongfully accused. Every day I went to that office and tried to cut through the red tape to find him. I spoke in Spanish to the officials, demanded attention, waited in offices, cried tears of frustration, until I was finally informed of his whereabouts and allowed to go and see him. I went and petitioned to see "my husband." I doubt if any of those

Arab officials had ever seen a young American woman with such tenacity and such devotion to her mate.

When I finally got to see and talk to Ron it was on a balcony right outside the cells. It was in the open air and very informal. Maybe a guard was present but if so, he was unobtrusive. Ron and I hugged and talked freely in English, which would not be understood if anyone was listening. Ron said he was treated well, the food was good and the accommodations were clean. The Arab guards were not as sadistic as American jail guards were, he said. Now I realized he had been in jail in America.

The Arab culture was very male-friendly, that is, the real friendships were between men. Overt homosexuality was frowned on, even illegal, although men friends held hands with each other and publicly showed each other affection. That behavior was accepted in their culture and not considered homosexual, as it would be in the United States. Women were considered less than men. Wives cooked and cleaned and had babies but were not friends with their husbands. Their women friends provided emotional and intellectual support. I'm sure there were affectionate and deep relationships between women, but we knew no women, because they were very sheltered. I had spoken to some Arab family women at the well near our house and sensed the bond between them. We had small talk, but there was no opening for deeper conversations.

The judicial process moved ahead and at the hearing the judge made his decision: we would have to leave the country at once. There was no fine or prison term, or trial, and that was a relief. I threw the coins for an I Ching reading and received "splitting apart," that seemed appropriate, but I wondered if it meant splitting apart for Ron and me. I felt out of my depth in our relationship. I loved him dearly, but I did not feel I was on his intellectual level.

After Ron was released we rented a room in a house at the top of a hill in the Casbah, far away from the old neighborhood where Benny and his cohorts reigned supreme. We were planning to leave the country, but we also knew the officials were not going to track us to see that we did. We were directly across the street from a café where music was played all day and most of the night. We spent a lot of time there, drinking mint tea, nibbling pastry and absorbing the mesmerizing rhythms and melodies of the music.

Our house was just down the street from where Barbara Hutton lived when she was in Tangier. We saw the wealthy American heiress a few times in the street. She was a slender, modest woman who did not flaunt her wealth. We were impressed that she had a house in the Medina rather than the European section. We were inside her house one time for a party when she was not in town. There were beautiful, colorful tiles on the floors and lovely tapestries on the walls.

Our motley crew of American and European friends continued to consult the I Ching for advice and spiritual guidance. Once, one of our mates was overstimulated and unsatisfied with his reading from that good book. He went to Barbara Hutton's residence and knocked on the door. When someone opened the door he threw the book inside and stalked off—an act of total cognitive dissonance.

Our next step was to move us to the European section

of town. A whole group of our American and European friends came with us. We rented a modern apartment with a real bathroom, a sit-down toilet, sink, tub and shower. The kitchen was fully equipped with an oven and a refrigerator; the beds were on a bedframe, off the floor. We were planning to leave Morocco, but we took our time.

Someone in our group had heard of a diet drug called "Maxiton Fort," an amphetamine that was sold over the counter at pharmacies. "Sallie can get it for us," someone suggested. "She can say she's on a diet if anyone asks." No one asked. I showed up, a very thin, American girl who spoke Spanish, seemed confident, and purchased a box of this drug. The drug was sold in ampules to be injected with a syringe. Who, besides us beatniks was using this? Wealthy Arab women? They would be the only people on a diet.

Well, we all got high on this new chemical substance. Another initiation for me: to inject a drug. I trusted Ron implicitly and he did it for me. I loved the high: a deep wave of intense physical pleasure flowed over my body, followed by a feeling of having lots of energy. The guys talked all night about writers, art, and the grand scheme of things. I had no desire to talk; I wanted to do something physical. I scrubbed the bathroom until the porcelain gleamed. I washed every dish after every use. Not that we ate a lot, the drug destroyed your appetite. We were young and reckless and thought we were on the cutting edge.

We made plans to go to London and bought marijuana pressed into thin squares to smuggle across the border. As the lone woman in the group and supposedly less suspicious, I was the designated smuggler and would carry the stuff in my underpants. I wasn't afraid. I had faith in the goodness of the world, my guardian angel, and felt my companions would never desert me. Looking back now, I think I was somewhat mad.

We left Morocco and successfully crossed the border into Spain via the ferry to Algeciras. Throughout my life, up until this time, I felt like I was in charge of what I did. In high school, I pursued academics while my dear neighborhood friends pursued vocations. They married, I went to college. My aptitude was mathematics, but I also took classes in Shakespeare, philosophy, and political science. I was influenced by my dad politically, but I went further and against his wishes, joined the Young People's Socialist League, the youth section of the Norman Thomas Socialist Party. I marched to the beat of my inner drummer—it was not the usual path taken.

After college I worked and lived at home to save money for a European trip with my best friend, Lynda. I was planning adventures and was open to new ideas and happenings. Meeting Ron and his bohemian compatriots put a halt to my planning. It was my choice then to follow along, and follow I did. I, who had been independent and would another day be so again, assumed the traditional female role of cook and helpmeet. What my lover and our group of male companions wanted of me I did. It was fearless and foolhardy, but I was hooked. Sex and drugs, the scourge of righteous and wholesome youthfulness had led me astray.

It was my path and I trod on it.

I have no regrets.

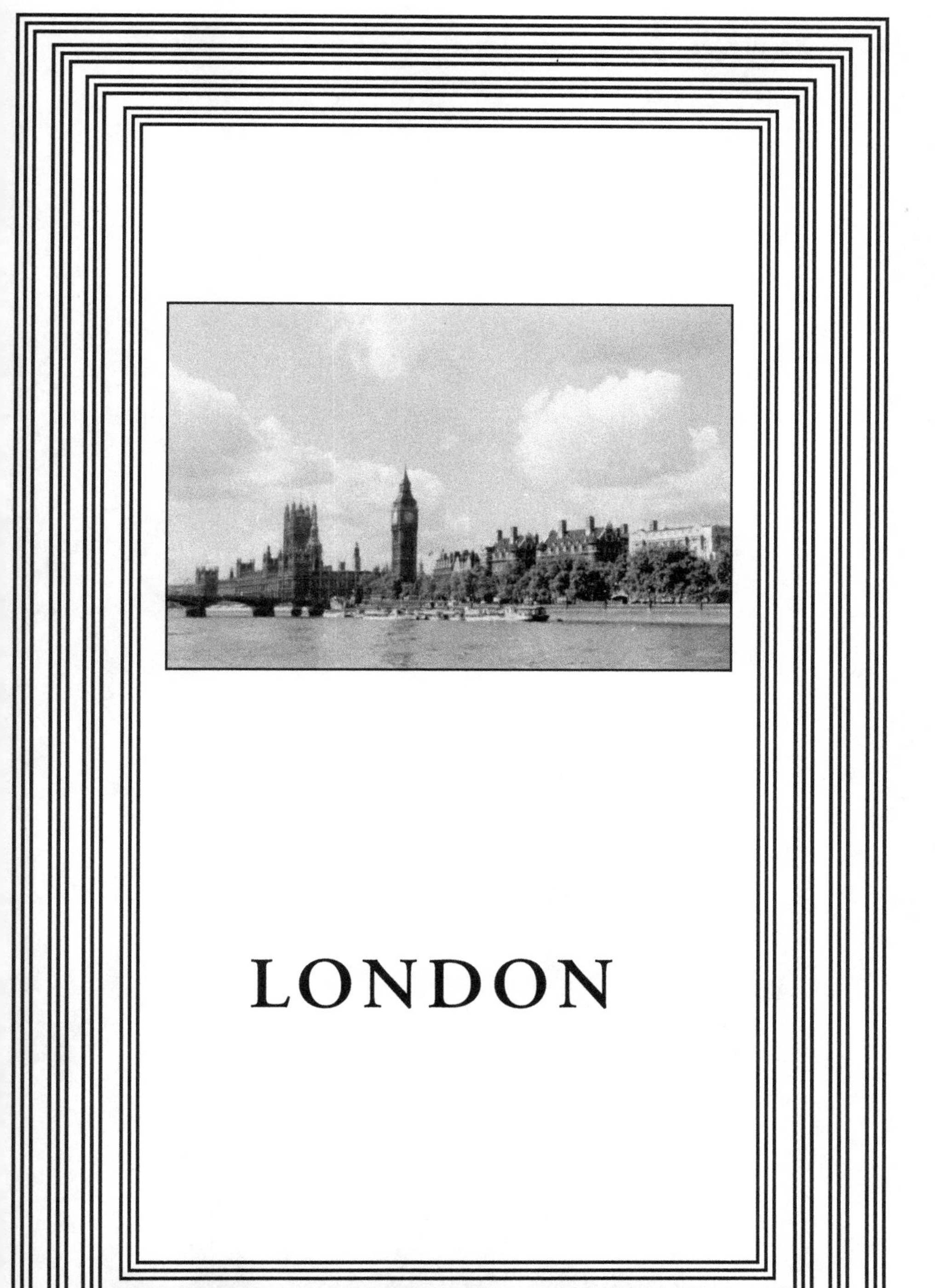

LONDON

Moving to London

We crossed the border into Spain without incident. No one suspected that I, the appointed smuggler, had pressed marijuana squares in my underpants. We took a train to Malaga and there I fell sick. I had no appetite, no energy for three days. When I tried to eat or drink, nothing stayed down, so I stayed in bed in our pensión. Ron was wise in these matters and noticed my yellow eye-whites: jaundice, possibly infectious hepatitis. We thought back to living in the European section apartment with four others. Everything was spanking clean compared to the Casbah places we lived in, but we shared a sit down toilet and ate together with our compadres. If anyone had hepatitis, it was easy to pass it around.

After three days I felt well enough to travel, so Ron and I pressed on together, our friends had already left. France was a blur on the train to the channel crossing. We took the boat to England and went through customs without a problem. Later I realized how lucky I was not to have been searched. Friends of ours in London were busted for pot and subsequently went to jail for years. Heroin and cocaine were available on the National Health Plan but having marijuana was an egregious offense.

Ron made an appointment for me to see a doctor. This kind man took one look at my jaundiced eyes and called an ambulance. I protested but he was adamant. I was hospitalized in the infectious ward, alone in a room with glass walls, not permitted to get up even to use the bathroom. After a few days I would sneak out to the restroom taking care to wash down the toilet seat. The bedpan was too humiliating. The doctors told me about hepatitis, a disease of the liver. To strengthen that organ the cure was bed-rest and an animal-fat free diet. The liver is where animal fats are digested and the liver needs to rest. The only meat they provided for me in the hospital was lean chicken breast; all other animal fats were proscribed. Years later in California, I conveyed this information to two friends at different times. These friends had hepatitis B and couldn't shake it. Their American doctors gave them no dietary advice but when they adopted the animal-fat free diet, they recovered.

Ron visited me every day. I was touched by his attention, his caring, his tenderness. I loved him dearly. I was not a coöperative patient to the hospital staff. They would not let me wash my hair, and my reaction was to hide under the covers of the bed and not show myself or answer questions. Eventually they let me wash my hair. I began to feel my strength and energy return after several days. My eye-whites were no longer yellow, and I felt I could handle my recovery on my own, so I discharged myself after eight days against the wishes of my doctor. I appreciated the care I had received for free, but I was headstrong and determined to be back with Ron.

My lover had rented a simple room in a house in Ladbroke Grove. It had a bed, a stove, a sink, and a chest of drawers all crammed into a small space. We shared a bathroom with the other tenants. Ron always found the hip place to live. This neighborhood was bustling with the Portobello outdoor market a block away. There was a fruit and vegetable market every weekday and antiques on the weekend.

The reason we had come to London was so Ron could get heroin and cocaine on the National Health Plan. He knew who to contact: Lady Frankau, an aristocrat and a psychiatrist, who prescribed these drugs to any and all comers who claimed to be addicted. Most, like Ron, had been addicted before and wanted to try the clean stuff dispensed by a doctor instead of street smack. Lady Frankau obliged and Ron began his journey. I didn't judge or condemn the drug use. I suppose it was like my dad's drinking when I lived at home. We didn't approve of it, in fact my mother and brothers and I hated it, but we could do nothing about it. As a child I accepted my parents, the whole package, infirmities as well as strengths. I keenly wanted Dad to stop drinking, but I did not feel responsible for it. Ron's drug use did not interfere with his loving relationship to me at this time. He was very tender in his affections. I was bedazzled.

Heroin satisfies the appetite for food and sex, as I found out, trying to heal us both with the delicious vegetable dishes I prepared. I loved the different veggies available at the market, especially rutabagas and parsnips. I bought a cookbook and tried to tempt Ron and his buddies with my creations. I had no success. If Ron was kind enough to try something, it didn't stay down, so that was a lost cause. I did discover the only food these junkies craved was sweets. So I made desserts; pineapple upside-down cake was my speciality.

Ron and I spent hours alone in the room on the bed reading aloud to each other. He was now interested in Buddhism and Eastern thought. We loved the sound of the names and designations: Avaloketishvara, Bodhisattva, Mahayana, Hinayana. This was music to my ears after William Burroughs. A lapsed Christian, I was fascinated and comforted by these readings. Ron and his cohorts also had tales to tell of Lenny Bruce. Ron could recite some of his skits and that kept me laughing.

My dear one had little interest in sex now that he was strung out, but he spent hours fondling me, trying to kindle the sex drive of his repressed mate. One day he asked me to marry him. I was amazed. He was a guru to me, teaching me about my body, about Eastern lore, about life and drugs. I had not thought about marrying him but I said: "Yes, yes and yes!" This was something I could write home about. After so much prevarication, I would finally tell my parents some of the truth. They had suspected something and were relieved.

We went to the Registry Office with two Americans who were our witnesses. They were Lynda's friends visiting London, and she had written me with their contact information. After the short civil ceremony, I invited them to our place for dinner. I was somewhat embarrassed that we were so poor, but they could see I was happy.

Both sets of parents sent congratulations in the form of cash, which was welcome as we were nearly broke. I suppose my parents thought we were sightseeing, or living an artist's existence; they never would have imagined the drug scene we inhabited.

We moved to less expensive digs around the corner. This place had a coal fireplace and a hot plate to cook on. That winter, 1962-1963, was one of the coldest in London's history. The pipes froze in our building and we had to get water from a faucet that the city set up on the street.

Ron was very thin now, even gaunt and haggard looking. His six foot four and half frame was never well padded, and now he was underweight. His fellow addicts all had that lean, hungry look, including Chet Baker, the jazz trumpeter. When Chet came with the group to fix at our place he wanted the limelight. We sat and watched as he slowly and dramatically tied off his arm, injected himself and sank into a chair with a look of satisfaction as the heroin flooded his body. We all felt sad that he was losing his embouchure, the shape of his lips, as he pursued the habit rather than play music and sing. Chet went on to make more records, but he never kicked his habit.

Lady Frankau fancied herself the healer of addicts, but she was not. She did nothing to help people understand why they needed and wanted to be addicted. There was a lot of pain in all these folks. A psychiatrist, Lady Frankau did not seem to realize the power of the mind to drive people to self-destructive behavior. She had no ability or desire to talk them through their pain and help them come up with other solutions.

Ron had told me something about his childhood traumas. His mother, a talented classical singer and an alcoholic, would scream at him and beat him with a coat hanger for some naughtiness and then break down crying and hug him closely, apologizing profusely for her outburst. This happened regularly when he was a little boy. Then his father divorced his mother and remarried. Ron thought his stepmother didn't like him; he thought that she gave him a room over the garage, because she didn't want him living in the house with her children.

I realized that Ron, like my father, had not experienced unconditional love from his parents. He was in pain and as intelligent and perceptive as he seemed to me, he needed drugs to staunch his misery. I did not see at the time that Ron was very much like my dad and that was a large part of the attraction for me. I was sympathetic to Ron's plight as I had been when Daddy told me stories of his youth.

I always accompanied Ron to his appointments with Lady Frankau and one day she called me into her office by myself. "I know you are using," she said. I wasn't but I knew Ron would be pleased to have more. "How much do you need?" The Lady inquired.

"A grain a day," I replied.

"Some cocaine with that?"

"Sure."

She was a piece of work.

When Ron started using heroin I asked him if I could try it; I was curious. "Sure," he said and injected me with a taste. It made me sick to my stomach. "Oh, yes," he informed me, "the first few times you get sick before the high kicks in." No thanks, I thought; getting sick on the way to paradise was a contradiction to me.

It was an enigma to me, why Ron and these others chose this drug. I knew it soothed their pain, and they all had psychological pain, existential pain. I didn't have that, but I did have a need to be loved and share a life with someone. I was out of my depth in this mad drug culture, but I needed and wanted to be with Ron. He and his fellow addicts experienced rapture from that drug; my rapture was living with the man I loved.

London, England-Winter 1962

I didn't do a lot of pondering about what was happening: the drug scene, the fact that Ron was now addicted to heroin, that I was married to him albeit in a very unconventional lifestyle. No, what I remember was living in the present moment, not knowing what would happen next, not being apprehensive. Up until meeting Ron I was inventing my life. Now I was following; I was passive. I did what was necessary to keep us afloat in the ocean of events that billowed over us.

As easily as Lady Frankau gave out heroin and cocaine, she took it away when she deemed it necessary. A few months of bliss, then wham, with no discussion or preparation, she informed Ron that she was cutting him down and off. Our English friends could enter a nursing home and take the methadone-sleep cure. Doctors administered methadone and narcotics to wean them off heroin. Most stayed clean for a while and then would re-apply for heroin.

Ron was not eligible for this help because he was American, not English, and he panicked. He went to another doctor while Lady Frankau was cutting him down. He gave the new doctor a name similar to his own and provided the same address. Busted. The National Health scrutinized the scripts as they went through the pharmacies, and he was arrested. Once again my mate was in jail. After a judge presented evidence in a non-public hearing, Ron was incarcerated at Brixton Prison.

Ron was a major player within our group of friends. His height, his experience, and his verbal skills commanded a leadership role in that circle. To his buddies, I was Ron's "old lady" and that carried weight and respect. They wanted to help. The plan was for me to carry some pills of methadone in a balloon in my mouth. When I visited him if we kissed I could pass it to him. I agreed without a blink of an eye.

I remember the gates of that prison as large and ominous, but I was not intimidated. I kept the balloon on one side of my mouth as I explained to the guards and the officials that my husband was there, and I very much wanted to see him. Once again my innocent appearance and genuine concern was my ticket. Ron and I met in a room with a guard at the door. We talked at a table and then kissed good-bye. Mission accomplished. He could now have some relief as he kicked his habit.

I was not aware that I was anxious as I carried out this dangerous mission. If I had been caught I would have been arrested. Like the smuggling, I did it because it was my job, and I must not have seemed nervous. But the anxiety was there under the surface of my conscious mind. There was more stress to come before it finally broke through the surface and caused a physical problem.

A few weeks later Ron was released and ordered to leave the country. We were ready to go and made plans. The night before we were to buy our plane tickets a "friend" came over. He was not one of our close comrades, but he needed a place to stay and Ron said he could. Before we retired, I saw Ron put our cash money in a bowl on the shelf near the stove. The guy staying saw that too. I never asked Ron if he expected our guest to steal the money, but he did steal it. Now we were broke. Both of us telegrammed our parents, and they came through. They wired us money, and we flew to

New York on Icelandic Airlines.

Being in my parents' house in Brooklyn with Ron was strange. I was on tenterhooks not knowing if the truth of Ron's drug addiction would come out. As usual, I continued to contribute to his dependency by getting him a drug he said he needed to help him sleep. We had taken Doradin, a tranquillizer, recreationally in London. We took it in the afternoon, wide awake and then got a high not unlike being drunk. I went to a neighborhood doctor and claimed to have used it for insomnia and procured a prescription. Ron's sleeplessness and general malaise were eased.

I could tell my dad didn't like Ron and my mother was skeptical. Nonetheless they were glad of the official marriage, and my uncle took the requisite photographs; the setting was the billiard table in my brothers' room. Mother hosted a shower where friends came and gave us presents, mostly money. Our Brooklyn community was generous.

Ron received news from his father that he had inherited a goodly sum of money. He decided that we would go back to Morocco right away. We booked passage on the Yugolinea Freight Lines. They had a bargain rate for a small group of passengers: $100 from New York to Casablanca.

There were fifteen or so of us passengers crammed into a few rooms on the small ship. We found ourselves with compatible young people seeking adventures in Morocco and experimenting with drugs. Someone had a supply of Librium and we all partook. It was a tranquilizer and made us very silly in the middle of the day or night. It didn't do much for my seasickness. I spent a lot of time heaving the greasy fare we were served into the deep. I finally stopped eating and just drank tea.

We had gatherings every night and generally acted out like teenagers. In the dining room the tables and chairs literally moved across the floor with the waves, and this was cause for great hilarity.

On the last night of the ten-day ordeal, we had a particularly rowdy party in someone's cabin, and the captain came barging into the room to reprimand us. One passenger had a dog, which promptly bit the Captain on the leg. He had to leave to the sound of our half-suppressed laughter.

The next day before we landed, the captain, red-faced and sputtering, called us to the dining room to lecture us about appropriate passenger behavior. "I am the Captain." He spit out, "I am in charge!" He was right of course, but his high-handed self-importance did not convince us. We continued to giggle behind his back.

Patsy — Tangier 1962

Ah, back in Morocco...warm weather and exotic fragrances. We hitchhiked from Casablanca to Tangier where we rented a room in a house in the Medina near the beach. We shared this house with other people, two of whom were Patsy and Fred. Patsy was English, six feet tall, thin, and willowy. She had long, blond-brown hair and a lovely face. Patsy had a compassionate aura about her. You felt she cared for you when you conversed with her. She was an earth mother.

Fred was taller and handsome with a dark beard. He was American, and later we would meet up with him and Patsy in San Francisco and become very good friends. Fred was a writer, and he taped his pages of work to the wall so you could walk in and peruse his latest. Patsy was an excellent cook, and I remember we had delicious meals in their room. I still eat her peanut butter and banana sandwiches today.

The house we lived in had a rooftop where women washed and dried their clothes and cooked their food. There was a faucet set low on a wall, and the women squatted over a basin to wash their laundry. They hung the wash to dry on a line and cooked in a charcoal bowl on the ground, also squatting. The view from the roof was spectacular: the turquoise Mediterranean Sea with its glowing white beaches and the decorative minarets of the mosques rising above the rooftops where Imams called the faithful to prayers five times a day.

None of Ron's old buddies were around, and it didn't seem to us that anything was happening, so we took the ferry to Spain. Once again I became sick, this time with "la grippe." I had a lot of pain in my back, so much so that I ran though the streets to the clinic I had seen, crying when I got there: *"Mucho dolor, mucho dolor!"* Those lovely people gave me a shot of morphine, and I awoke happily dazed. I had no more pain, and I was glad to see Ron standing by ready to take me back to the pensión where we were staying. I recovered, and we returned to Tangier to take the Yugolinea freighter back to New York, this time without incident.

Now we were ready to go to the left coast. Ron's home was Los Angeles.

Sallie and Ron — Brooklyn 1963

SAN FRANCISCO

Summer 1963 - 24 Years Old

Back in Brooklyn, we stayed briefly with my parents while Ron searched the newspapers for a ride-share drive across the country. He found one, and we set off on the iconic California trip. It was almost non-stop driving between Ron and the car owner. I slept in the back seat or talked to whoever was driving, I did not drive at the time. We undoubtedly took the northern route, as it was the summer and too hot for the southern route. It was all a blur to me. I do remember stopping in Reno and playing a slot machine for the first and only time in my life. As soon as I won, I quit.

It was not a foggy day as we drove into San Francisco from the Bay Bridge. The sun was drenching the hills with white California light. The Bay sparkled and the air was breezy and clean. The city was reminiscent of European cities: small streets, houses climbing up the hillsides, spectacular views of the Pacific Ocean, the Golden Gate Bridge, Mount Tamalpais, sailboats on the bay. This was a place we could settle into, especially when we saw the young men growing their hair long as Ron had started to do.

But first we needed to visit Ron's family in Los Angeles. We bussed to Southern California for the obligatory family reunion and to introduce me. Ron was not excited by the idea but felt it was necessary. Ron's dad was glad to see him and meet me, but Ron disliked his stepmother, so he did not enjoy the visit. He went to see his mother without me. I didn't ask why but knew it was because he could have a more intimate conversation without me.

In contrast to San Francisco, L.A. was huge and sprawling, a continuous suburb with no center throbbing with activity. The freeways were clogged with people in their vehicles looking none too happy. This was not for us; we took a bus back to San Francisco after a few days.

We found a furnished apartment on Leavenworth Street bordering on Chinatown. It was a one-room place with a Murphy bed that folded down from a wall, a tiny kitchen, and bathroom. It was a residential neighborhood near the cable car. I was charmed by the Asian children I saw playing in the streets and nearby park. They were active but so quiet. One child would hide from another and then jump out to playfully scare the friend; both reacted joyously with hardly a sound—very different from the noisy Brooklyn streets of my childhood.

I started to look for work downtown, thinking now maybe we could live a normal life in this beautiful city. Ron had a monthly inheritance check and didn't seem interested in seeking employment. He diddled around with his writing, and we went to the movies a lot. In retrospect, I think that seeing his parents and his stepmother again triggered painful memories he felt helpless to deal with. We were no longer in an exotic country with its distractions, or in England where he could self-medicate with heroin. We were at home, and home is where his heart was broken. His general lethargy and depressed mental states were new to me. He had always been active, even as a drug addict we did things, we went to see people, we had people over to our place, we read books, and talked of ideas.

I found a job in an insurance company as a clerk; I

was unsure of my career plan. What did I really want to do? My interest in math and science had waned and nothing had taken its place. We didn't know anyone yet and the nascent hippie scene didn't extend to us at that time. We floundered. Ron started drinking, and his disposition soured even more. He started to abuse me verbally. "You're not sensitive," he would say. "You don't know what's going on." I was flabbergasted and just listened without defending myself. My mother had put up with similar attacks, and I followed suit.

One evening to my surprise, (I was so naïve) the verbal abuse turned physical. Ron had been drinking, and he punched me in the face. I was shocked and frightened, and put up no defense except cowering on the floor. Immediately he fell to his knees and begged forgiveness. Sobbing, he rued his attack and held me tenderly, almost exactly as he had told me his mother had acted with him as a child. Of course at the time I didn't remember that. I was dumbstruck, catapulted back to my personal hallucination: thinking I was my mother when we first had sex.

After another incident like that, Ron sought help from a psychiatrist. We both went, me with a black eye, he repentant and remorseful. The doctor tried to help, but it must have involved a commitment to stop drinking, because Ron didn't pursue that course of action. The doctor offered me no advice. I was under Ron's influence and just accepted his decisions. I continued to work at my job and befriended a woman co-worker. I liked this woman, but I didn't confide in her.

After another assault, I called her and asked if I could spend the night at her place. She said yes, so I left a note for Ron that I was leaving. I made the mistake of telling him where I was going. He showed up looking fearsome, but I dutifully followed him back to our place. There he took off his belt and hit me several times before collapsing in sorrow and anguish. "I don't want to hurt you," he pleaded, "I can't help myself." He snuggled me for a long time, apologizing and murmuring how much he loved me and how he wanted to do right by me. His tenderness won me over and I melted into his arms. When I tried to get up for my diaphragm, he convinced me that at this time in my menstrual cycle I wouldn't need protection. He knew my cycle, and once again I foolishly accepted his judgment. Wrong. I got pregnant. My body ached for a child, but now I knew for sure that Ron was not the father I wanted for my baby. Abortion was illegal at this time; doctors could be imprisoned for performing one. Back-alley procedures were available and very dangerous for women. It was a quandary for me.

As I remember it, I was rather stoical about my problem. Like my Scottish mother I thought I was an independent woman, but like her when it came to the relationship of husband and wife I fell back to the traditional role of serving and putting my desires aside to follow my husband. My desires for the future were not defined at this point. I just wanted to get through the day, to persevere as a loyal wife and helpmeet. This was all I was capable of at this point. The bond of sex was very strong. Later when I read Simone de Beauvoir's book *The Second Sex*, I saw myself as she wrote about abused women who stay with their partners because of that physical tie.

I drank bottles of castor oil, which were nauseating

and ineffective. I sat in a hot bathtub every night to no avail. Ron told me of his friend Tibor in New York City, who could help me out. Ah, New York City, I could escape to my hometown and start over.

This was all happening in the fall of 1963; I was 24 years old. I had another job at that time in a stock firm. I did paperwork at a desk while the ever-present ticker-tape machine clicked away. On November 22, I was doing my job in the afternoon when the ticker-tape machine stopped. Everyone looked up. That sound was on-going; it never stopped. After a few minutes some garbled messages began to filter through and eventually we learned that President Kennedy had been shot in Dallas. We were dismissed for the day, and I rode the cable car home. Everyone was crying and moaning and talking to each other in grief. To me it was a terrible thing to happen, but I was far too involved in my personal problems to follow the public tragedy. I had to get to New York and find Tibor.

Somehow I put the money together to buy a ticket and flew to my home city. On arriving at my parents' home in Brooklyn I learned that my mother was in the hospital with breast cancer. She had discovered a lump and the doctors decided on a radical mastectomy for her right breast. She was glad to see me, maybe she thought Daddy had called me, but she never asked me the reason for my visit. I did not mention my dilemma and did what I could to comfort her. My dear mother was not big on accepting sympathy or assistance, so I plunged into my quest for Tibor and an abortion.

Ron had informed his friend of my need and Tibor was ready to help. He arranged for us to go to the

Pennsylvania town where a well-known doctor practiced. I visited my great friend Lynda in Manhattan, told her my problem, and asked for a loan. She graciously gave me $500 without batting an eye. Lynda was following her life path, a more mainstream way of life than mine. She was seeing Frank, her boyfriend; she had a job as a computer programmer for IBM, and she rented a New York apartment with a roommate on the Upper East Side. Lynda was, and still is, a real friend to me. She never judged my actions, never plied me with advice. She was concerned for me and would do whatever I needed to help me.

Tibor and I arrived in the sleepy little town where nothing was happening except the abortionist's practice. The townspeople were conservative and generally disapproved of this business, but they enjoyed the benefits of a steady stream of visitors to hotels, motels, and restaurants, so they did not protest. When I got to the office door there was a sign that said "Dr. X has retired." Not deterred, I pushed the door open and found a busy, friendly clinic in progress. After examining me the doctor said he would help me, but had I come a week later he would not have; I would have been too far along. I was grateful.

He was pleasant, efficient, and thorough. I awoke to see Tibor and the doctor smiling at me. I was given pills to prevent milk, pills to prevent infection, and pills for pain. We drove back to New York, where I stayed with Lynda for a few days. When I went back to Brooklyn my mother was at home, and my dad had his drinking under control for the time being. He was very shook up by my mother's illness and did his best to ease the situation.

I had a nervous reaction to the strain of these events. My whole body was feeling the "pins and needles" response as when a leg or foot "falls asleep." The edge of my skin everywhere was experiencing electrical tingling—not very pleasant. I sought help from a woman doctor Lynda recommended. She told me I was anemic and prescribed medicine. She thought the tingling was nerves, and I should try to relax.

Ron began calling every day to inquire about my health and well-being. He was very concerned and begged me to consider returning to California. He had a job now with the Post Office and had rented a charming house on a hill in the Mission District. He missed me terribly and wanted to make amends for his egregious behavior. I wavered for weeks, but his persistence won out. He sent me a ticket and I returned. The ironic result was that in stepping off the plane and seeing him the tingling sensations disappeared.

Ron's power prevailed over my body.

Starting Over 1964-1965

A new chapter of our marriage began. Ron was working at the Post Office, and he had rented a lovely wood-frame house in the Mission District. The remorse he felt after abusing me, and my flight to New York had propelled him into his better self. He eschewed hard drugs and was thrilled that I returned to be with him. I was very glad to be the recipient of his positive energy and love.

I got a job more in line with my qualifications at Pacific Bell. Based on my experience at Bell Labs, this was a managerial position but not on electronic research. I was now a traffic engineer, I read reports of suburban growth and estimated how many trunks of telephone wires would be required to accommodate that growth. Not as much fun as hooking up circuits and using the fluxmeter, but I was grateful for the chance to use my intelligence and be well paid. The other traffic engineers were mostly women, lovely people, and I made work friends.

Ron and I were now gathering a social circle. When we lived on Leavenworth Street our good luck was to have Fred Rohé as our mailman—the Fred we knew from Tangier, married to Patsy. Fred recognized Ron's name on the mailbox and knocked on our door. In the turmoil of those days on Leavenworth Street, when Ron was depressed and mistreated me, we had not made contact, but now we did. It was a serendipitous connection that brought us four together again. Ron felt comfortable with Fred and Patsy and so did I. Those three people were all over six feet tall, but I didn't feel odd being five feet four. We all felt change in the air, it was a time of new consciousness rising. Not only were we a new generation; we saw the world in a different way. Like the Beats we were not interested in material goods or living high on the hog; we wanted to explore our inner life, discover our true selves, our natural selves. We wanted to find nirvana!

Marijuana was our drug of choice, and it fostered social relationships and friendly behavior. Ron was relaxed and treated me well. He made gentle love to me and was attentive to my needs. We listened to Bob Dylan and the San Francisco bands: the Jefferson Airplane, the Grateful Dead, the Quicksilver Messenger Service and the Charlatans, these groups were singing about love and coming together.

We lived as a couple and felt communally attached to our friends and the growing hippie scene. We dressed casually and colorfully. We rejected middle class conventions; we had a mattress on the floor for our bed, a kitchen table and chairs, mats on the floor instead of couches and chairs in the living room. We had a radio and a record player with a few records. We were attracted to Zen Buddhism and our uncluttered house décor reflected the Zen style that "less is more."

We lived on Bernal Hill and had friends, Bob and Ellen, who lived nearby. One Sunday morning they called to say they had decided to tie the knot formally, and asked if we would accompany them on their quest to get married. Yes! We piled into Bob's old car and went to two churches and a synagogue. What a surprise to find that no one would marry them: "You must be a member of the church. You must have two weeks counseling."

At the end of the afternoon, we were disappointed and discouraged. Then someone had an idea: to go to the San Francisco Zen Center. We had all been there for meditation and we revered Suzuki Roshi. Off we went. The receptionist sent us upstairs to wait outside his door. Wait we did, patiently for a long time, at least an hour. Finally he called us to come in. He was seated at a low table, cross-legged on a chair with some calligraphy before him. He greeted us, and Ellen explained their mission and our disappointments. "We want someone to be spontaneous," she said.

"I am spontaneous in my refusal," he replied.

We all laughed. Ellen and Suzuki Roshi continued talking while Ron and I melted into the background. After a while Ellen said, "I want you to marry us whenever you wish."

"Fine," said Suzuki Roshi, "come back at 8 o'clock."

We were overjoyed.

He performed the elaborate ceremony in Japanese with chanting and waving of scarves. It was beautiful. We loved him very much.

* * *

At this time, I went to a doctor to get birth control pills. This made my life easier, and I felt safer about avoiding pregnancy since the control was in my hands. Ron teased me when I posted my calendar on the kitchen cabinet; the calendar was for ticking off the pill days. "Now anyone who helps themselves to a glass of water can see your menstrual cycle!"

I also went to an ophthalmologist to be fitted for contact lenses. I was very myopic and had to wear glasses since I was 10 years old. When I didn't wear my glasses,

I was living in the fuzzy world. My cornea was the right shape and the hard lenses of the time felt fine. I was amazed to see the world through lenses directly on my eyes rather than through glasses inches from my eyes. The volume of things was larger, and when I looked in the mirror I could see my face clearly without glasses. I saw the resemblance to my mother, whereas all my life I was told I looked like my father. These changes made me feel more confident and happy.

Ron was from Los Angeles, and cars had always been a part of his life. He now owned an old-fashioned 1940's model. It was sturdy and he sometimes drove rather recklessly at night up and down the San Francisco hills. He was showing off his skill, but it wasn't my idea of fun. I had no desire to learn to drive, another thing I had in common with my mother who never learned. Mother was very proud of me when years later I conquered my fear and learned to drive at age forty. Ron also loved motorcycles, and at one point had a Black Vincent bike. He showed it off and talked endlessly about it to fellow motorcycle enthusiasts. We had one helmet that he would wear when we tore up the freeway at high speeds with me clutching his back. I had total faith in his ability and his love for me and never felt we would crash or turn over. Life was a big adventure, and I was an avid participant. I was enjoying myself now that we had a somewhat normal life, and Ron was in a good mood.

Our friend Gordon, from Tangier, came to San Francisco and we delighted in the reunion. Gordon was friends with a potter who lived in St Helena, an hour ride north of our city. Jack Sears was married to Mardi Wood, also a fine pottery maker. We visited them in

Jack Sears — 1964

Sonoma County and were entranced with the beauty of the landscape, their work, and Jack's dynamic personality. He was the natural, organic man. He made his own clay, his own glazes, and built his wheel and kiln from scratch. He had lived in Japan and was an admirer, if not a student of Zen Buddhism. He lived in his vision of connection to nature. His one pointed focus was to make beautiful, utilitarian pottery from the earth to the table to drink and eat with friends and family.

Ron was fascinated with Jack and his pottery and he started making pots using Jack's equipment. He did very well, even selling some of his creations. So Ron decided that we would move to St. Helena and make our life in that creative community. I had worked for Pacific Bell for six months and was not averse to change. It was a lovely world in that small town, and our friends were very welcoming. As a married woman, I was expected to follow my husband to his new location, so I qualified for unemployment insurance. I knew that was the last time I could work for the telephone company, but that did not bother me. My own creative powers were not fulfilled there, and big companies were not my desired workplace.

We packed up our few possessions, and off we went to Napa Valley and another life experience. We found a sweet little house for rent at the end of Sulfur Springs Road, near the Martini winery and a few minutes from Jack's studio. Ron went to Jack's every day. I bought a bicycle and trundled around doing errands till I rode over to the studio in the afternoon. I passed many vineyards on my rounds and watched the deepening color of the leaves from green to golden brown to rust in the fall and fluttering to the ground in the wet winter.

In the afternoons and evenings we would ceremoniously drink tea from the cups Jack would remove from the kiln, freshly made and glazed that morning. We smoked pot and drank a little wine. The wineries were generous and gave us open bottles from their tasting rooms. It rained a lot that winter, but we were cozy in our social circle; Jack and Mardi's studio was always toasty warm from the kiln and alive with people talking. We spoke of raku, stoneware, and porcelain, like metaphors for life: Raku for simplicity, stoneware, deeper complexity, and porcelain, the most complex but most fragile existence.

Ron was in his element and his pots were selling in

shops. I was pleased with my easy-going life and happy for him. He had an outlet for his creativity, and his relationship to Jack kept his substance abuse problem under control. Jack was a guru for Ron, and Jack needed no hard drugs. Ron kept learning from Jack and making his own pottery creations. But inevitably he became restless, he was a child of the city and so was I. We were curious about the happenings in San Francisco and after six months we moved back to our city.

We rented an apartment on Guerrero Street in the Mission district, and I pursued any job I could to make money. I still did not have an idea of what I would like to do. I worked as an invoice clerk for Baker and Hamilton, a hardware distribution warehouse. It was a depressing environment. The offices were above the unpaved warehouse space where the goods were stored, where large motorized trucks shifted the boxes of stuff around and into trucks. It was very dusty. You walked up a narrow staircase to the offices. Men and women sat at desks under dim lights to tally the products in and out. There was a lounge/restroom that had no particular style. It was a boxy room with nondescript couches. Everywhere a brownish haze hung in the air from the ground stirred up below.

In the midst of this dusky, gloomy place was a woman clerk who dressed every day in colorful, flamboyant clothes: taffeta dresses with wide skirts, bright red lipstick and pancake makeup. She looked as if she were going to a fancy ball in the 1940s. She must have been good at math to have the job, but her fantasy was palpable. It was sad to see her fooling herself that she had an exciting life.

We reconnected to Patsy and Fred, and things were happening in their life together. They had a son, Jason, and Fred had put together funds to buy The Sunset Health Food Store. Fred had a strong interest in health food and he planned to change this old-fashioned place with dusty shelves of vitamins and remedies into his vision of a new way of eating. He contacted farmers who grew organic produce, and soon there were boxes of fresh vegetables for sale. His passion was infectious, and we all became vegetarians. We read about macrobiotics and experimented with healthy diets. Fred kept a stick of margarine on his desk in the back of the store for years. It never changed, never decayed—Fred's example of plastic food. Later, I worked at the store and the transformation grew deeper: refrigerated shelving for fresh eggs, cheese, and yogurt, organic cosmetics. I loved the strawberry cleansing cream. He offered all the new books on health and health foods, and advertised lectures and workshops on healthy life styles. Fred renamed his store New Age Natural Foods. It was the prototype of all the future health food stores.

We were amazed by the proliferation of the hippie scene in the Haight Ashbury neighborhood. The year before there had been dozens of folks walking down the street into the park; now there were hundreds. The Psychedelic Shop offered pipes and all manner of paraphernalia for smoking and using pot, hash, and other goodies. Second hand clothing stores offered dress-up clothes and music stores sold the records of psychedelic rock 'n roll. Something was definitely happening here and we relished it.

Sallie and Ron — Muir Woods 1964

1965 Positive Distractions

We moved from the apartment on Guerrero to a back cottage in the Mission District. There was a garden between our place and the front house with flowers blooming. One was the beauteous opium poppy. When its bright red, papery petals fell off, the seedpods were plump with uncured opium. Of course Ron knew how to slit the pod, let the opium ooze out, and prepare it to smoke. Yes, drugs were finagling their way back into his life and consequently, mine. He was making connections to dealers in the Haight and was probably using heroin or cocaine. He was a troubled soul. He had tantrums like a child and started accusing me of poisoning his food. Once again, I was bamboozled and flustered by these absurd charges. He did not hit me, but I feared another disastrous episode could ensue. Ron must have felt scared too, because he consulted a psychiatrist. I went with him to meet a very empathetic woman doctor who was very interested in Ron. She diagnosed him as a paranoid schizophrenic and outlined a way how he could see her for very little money. Alas, he did not respond to her.

I was working at another dead end job; I was a bank teller at the Bank of America. The only good thing about it was I could walk to work. I had some work friends, and I remember one woman who had aspirations to rise from the ranks of teller to a managerial position. In banking at that time there were no women managers, and the men in those positions were condescending to women, even scornful of the idea of a woman boss. I could see the hopelessness of my friend's ambition, that she would not reach her goal. The powers that controlled advancement were too strong, too adamant, too dominant. Strange that I could not see the nowhere street I was on with Ron. I guess I thought of myself as in transition. I would eventually figure something out: a job that was right for me that I would pursue. Ron would settle down, or I would leave. I lived one day at a time and suffered the unhappy marriage like a martyr.

Ron's way of coping with a difficult situation was to change our physical location when things got really rough. He was very depressed at this time. He didn't want to see our friends, he moped, and sometimes lay on the floor in pain and spouted absurdities, like I was his enemy or everything and everyone was against him. At the same time he had his feelers out for another house to rent on Bernal Hill, and it was our good luck to find one just a few doors down from where we had lived before we left for St. Helena. It was a wooden frame house with two bedrooms. There had been some hippies living there before, and they painted on the bedroom wall: "Way out people know the way out." The last word was over the window that looked out to Twin Peaks and was twenty or so feet above the street—it meant suicide.

Those previous renters left behind a kitten, a dear sweet tabby. I was thrilled, I loved having a pet, and I had not had one since my childhood. Ron liked the kitten well enough, but he soon traded it to a friend for a full-grown cat, a longhaired orange male he dubbed Sam. Ron liked Sam because Sam walked on Ron's shoulders. Sam was our faithful companion through thick and thin over the next few years and my best buddy after we broke up.

We had a friend, Herb, who owned the Blue Unicorn Café in the Haight. Herb had many connections and invited us to go with him to Allen Ginsberg's Halloween Party where Captain America would make an appearance. We were excited to go and meet the great poet, Allen Ginsberg, who was then living on Fell Street. For the occasion, Allen took off all his clothes, his naked body his costume. Allen was hirsute, his dark hair was plentiful, and covered his body. Like a great fuzzy bear he greeted his guests with a friendly smile and twinkling eyes. I remember petting his shoulder and smiling at him. Allen loved people, and his warmth enveloped you. In one of the rooms, The Fugs, a New York band who played rock'n roll with crazy lyrics, was cookin' away while people danced.

Ah, dancing to the music here was something I loved. We were mostly stoned on pot and danced with each other, not holding a partner but as a group, emphasizing our communal feelings of joy, feeling the beat, and the theme of love. It was a spiritual experience of oneness with all. It transcended the mundane workaday existence. It suggested other ways of living without the conventional restrictions of social behavior. It felt like freedom.

The next dance event was a benefit for the San Francisco Mime Troupe at the Fire House Theater in downtown San Francisco. Ron and I had discovered the Mime Troupe in 1963 when they first started performing in the parks in the summertime. The troupe was not pantomime; there was hilarious dialogue. In those days it wasn't blatantly political, but more like an Italian Everyman play: exaggerated, expressive, often salacious words and over-stated body language. We loved this group and their benefit dance was packed with fans. We danced wildly and happily till the Fire Department closed us down for overcrowded conditions. We were disappointed, but we followed the orders to leave realizing there was a fire hazard with so many bodies crammed into a small space. Bill Graham, the manager of the Mime Troupe, was at that benefit dance and recognized the potential of a dance venue. People needed a place to let their hair down and express joy in life and music. He opened the Fillmore Auditorium a few months later.

I got a better job, although still a wage-slave position, at the Traveler's Insurance Company. I was a rate clerk who tallied accidents to the policies of car owners. The work was somewhat mathematical but also mechanical and dull. The work environment was oppressive: a huge room with desks and a supervisor in the back watching like a hawk. She would mark you down as late if you were not in your seat at your desk when the bell rang—a loud, clanging bell like an elementary school recess bell. Those unpleasant sounds also marked the ten-minute coffee breaks at mid-morning, mid-afternoon, and lunch time. You could accumulate tardy marks if you were standing, not sitting, at your desk at the appointed times.

The stacks of folders with your work were endless. Just when you finished a large pile and you started to feel a sense of accomplishment, another mound would appear. After several months I joined with a group of workers, mostly women, who were meeting with a union in the hopes of organizing the workplace and bettering our conditions. We had surreptitious encounters after work with the labor organizers, who were excited by the idea, but had to be cautious in their approach to this large corporate body that had so much power.

* * *

Our friend Herb told us about his friend, Neal Cassady, who was the model for the character Dean Moriarty in Jack Kerouac's book *On the Road.* Wildly energetic, Dean drove cars across the country seeking adventures, drugs, and women.

"You should meet him," Herb urged us, "invite him to dinner."

Fine we replied, telling Herb to extend the invitation. The next night we got a call from Neal.

"Please come over," I said, "we're having tongue."

"That's appropriate," said Neal.

I was mystified. Tongue was cheap, and I was a frugal shopper. Appropriate for what? I soon found out. Neal bounded up the stairs and into our lives like a cheerful, lively emcee. He talked non-stop, a stream of consciousness monologue, his thoughts bubbling forth: his life experiences, his opinions on everything, including the people present. Ron and I were speechless, very unusual for Ron, who was usually the center of the conversation. After a time, we realized he was talking about us.

"Are these people dumb? Do they have anything to say?"

Ron and I looked at each other askance. Then Ron jumped into the banter, and it became conversation.

"Ah," Neal opined, "I'm not in Deadsville, there's life here." And Neal gave us his blessing.

"These folks are cool, they're just overwhelmed by my babbling."

Neal was nothing if not perceptive and kind.

Neal liked us, and to our delight, he would drop in

unannounced. One evening he brought his girlfriend Ann. She sat quietly sewing a shirt for him.

"Wow," I thought. "She's like a handmaiden."

I didn't see my relationship to Ron like that. Neal was bursting his buttons, holding forth with his monologues, standing in front of our radio with KSAN rock'n roll accompanying him. He was friends with the Grateful Dead, and later we saw him at the Fillmore on the stage telling his stories with the Dead behind him. These social events, and our deepening involvement with the hippie culture were very good for Ron. He was happier and his own psychological problems took a back seat now. I too was entranced by these events and desirous of going along this path of music, dance, and community relationships. We were striving towards some of kind of enlightenment.

Sam — San Francisco 1966

1965 Continues

There was no Internet in the '60s, but there was a human web of connection in the counterculture. We had our newspapers: The *Oracle* was about spiritual experience and goals; The *Good Times* and the *Berkeley Barb* had some conventional news and information on the protests, marches, and rallies as well as articles on our music and ideas. Sometimes news was spread via the human grapevine. One Sunday morning, I was on Mission Street in San Francisco picking up groceries, and a guy I didn't know came up to me.

"The Cream," he said, "will be in the park today!"

That well-known English rock band in Golden Gate Park! A free concert? We were there.

One way or another we heard of the Sexual Freedom League. We never went to meetings, but we got the idea! If we were truly free we should be able to share sexual love with people other than our spouses or partners. Jealously was not a hip emotion, and we should test the waters and see if we could overcome possessiveness. I was open to the idea, not eager, but willing to try. There was a couple up the street, Ormond and Lisa, who were our age, smoked pot and were interested in ideas like sexual freedom as proposed by Jefferson "Fuck" Poland in his manifesto. We arranged an evening of exchange. I was surprised by the outcome. Ron had been my only lover, and when we had sex he was totally involved in my pleasure. Having sex with Ormond was very disappointing, because it was all about his pleasure. Other occasions had similar results, and I always ended up back in bed with Ron for the consummation of my pleasure.

This was an education for me. The person who pleased me most could also be my tormentor. Ron's split personality was most obvious here. In his tender side he put my pleasure above his; in his dark side he could abuse me. Later I read that many battered women faced this dilemma. In the meantime, I was glad that Ron's gentle side was then at the fore and our social activities were expanding.

* * *

One night I went with Neal on his rounds in his rattletrap jalopy. He was a car freak and knew all about the mechanics of cars, but having little money his vehicles were not the most comfortable. We bounced along till he came to his first destination. We dashed up the stairs and knocked; Neal always went at a fast pace. The door opened on a hippie pad with a dozen or so people sitting in a circle on the floor smoking pot. They were happy to see Neal and welcomed us both. Neal entertained us for an hour or so with his repartee, and then the two of us proceeded to the next place. I felt like I was on a movie set; it was dark outside and in the car, relatively quiet with Neal mumbling, then a door opens and there's light shining on a scene in a room with people getting high and talking avidly. Neal was the star. He relished being the star as much as he loved people and adventure.

Neal seemed to have boundless energy, but he supplemented his natural supply with various types of speed, cocaine, meth, Dexedrine, whatever he could get. He sniffed the drugs or ate them off the side of his hand. Pot was a given and LSD was a treat; he never turned down a high. Neal was lean and muscular. He looked healthy, but his eyes had dark circles and the look of sleep deprivation. He ate with anyone and everyone who invited him, but I'm sure his personal eating habits were irregular.

Years later, City Lights published his writings The First Third. In this book he recounts his childhood experiences in the Depression on the mean streets of Denver. Born in 1926, when he was six years old his meek, alcoholic dad took him to live in flophouses for a year. They scrounged for food, and Neal suffered greatly when his dad drank himself into a stupor. At that young age Neal managed to get himself to school and he learned to read. The descriptions of this tough environment are detailed and stark. Back with his mother and stepbrothers the next year his comfort level was a tad higher, but one brother tormented him. The whole family slept in a Murphy bed that pulled down from the wall. In the daytime his older brother Jack would lock him in the bed when it was secured against the wall. He could hardly breathe but suffered his treatment quietly.

One time in this childhood torture chamber, Neal had an unusual and scary experience. A buzz in his ear led to a speed up in his brain and time seemed to move very quickly. This happened to him again later, and he was puzzled by it. Of course Neal seldom if ever consulted a doctor, so he never found out if there was a scientific explanation for this phenomenon. These difficult circumstances, poverty, an alcoholic father, a mother too pressed with many children to give him the love he craved from her, a brother obsessed with hurting him, made him the man he was. To me it is amazing that he was so kind and good-hearted. The great communicator was always telling us everything in his mind and ready to hear our thoughts. Ironically, or maybe consequently, he died in Mexico in 1968 of "over-exposure." No one was as over-exposed as Neal.

Excitement was in the air in San Francisco. The counterculture was growing. The San Francisco bands were developing and playing all the time. We were dancing, getting stoned, and loving it. We heard about a new drug: LSD. Legal at this time, it could transport you to the highest ecstasy: nirvana, enlightenment, bliss consciousness. We were fascinated. Ron and I bought *The Psychedelic Experience*, a book by Leary, Alpert and Metzner, a manual for taking LSD based on the *Tibetan book of the Dead.* LSD would open the third eye and you would see things as they really were, unspoiled by social convention, egocentricity, and fear. We diligently read the book to prepare for a spiritual experience. This was different from grass (pot), which was sense enhancing and created a loving feeling towards others but fell short of providing the "Clear Light of Reality." Heroin produced a peaceful state at the expense of one's health. Cocaine, Methedrine, Dexedrine and other uppers we had taken were physical highs. LSD proposed to open a door to a new consciousness.

We procured our Sandoz acid, made in a scientific laboratory in New Jersey, and one Sunday morning Ron and I began our journey together. After twenty or so minutes I started to feel a deep peace and quietude. I remember smiling and feeling I could soar to another world. Just then I heard Ron moaning. He was resisting the awakening effects of LSD and falling into his misery.

He felt afraid, insecure, troubled, his childhood memories were pulling him down. Of course I comforted him. We lay on our bed together breathing, embracing. After holding him close and cooing to him for some time, I realized he was bringing me down. His influence over me was strong, but this time I turned over, away from him, and blacked out. Later someone told me this was a healthy thing to do, since he was dragging me with him into the mire.

Eventually I woke or Ron nudged me. His demons had passed and we discovered that I had peed on the bed. Ron thought this was charming and funny and we both laughed. It was time to get up. We made our way to the kitchen and ate something and played with Sam, our cat. It was getting dark. Ron, being in control of himself now, drove us to the beach. On walking through a tunnel we started to see flashing rainbow lights. When we stepped out to the sand everything was glowing in psychedelic radiance. The waves were shimmering with purple and green lights; the sky was gleaming with stars and a sparkling luminescence. The sand had a jewel-like quality, glittering. A soft breeze was blowing and all was right with the world.

The next day I was not interested in going to work at Traveler's Insurance Company. I called to say I was not feeling well, and since it was a cloudy day I was staying home. Later that week I was fired. "The weather is no excuse for staying home," I was told. Good. The job had been over for me months ago, and I was happy to be released.

Now, due to the stimulation of acid (LSD), I started to think about what job I would like to do. I realized that I wanted to be with children, but not have children with Ron. A teacher, a librarian, these were jobs I knew I could do and enjoy. I had been to the UC Berkeley campus. It was beautiful, and I could get a children's librarian degree there. San Francisco State was a well-reputed school for a teaching credential. I thought: "Do I want noise or quiet? A primary classroom or library room?" I opted for noise and enrolled at San Francisco State for an elementary teaching credential. I took the relevant classes: Children's Literature, Educational Psychology, Child Development, and Nature Study. In the Lit class, I wrote a paper comparing *Alice in Wonderland*, my favorite childhood book, with *Wind in the Willows*, which I read for the first time. *Wind in the Willows* was like a Zen story to me, things progressed slowly and gently. The lull of the river was soothing, the genteel English style comforting. It portrayed an easy-going and contented life with occasional outbursts by Toad. Next to that "Alice" seemed almost violent to me. Alice was harried, harassed by the March Hare, threatened by the Queen, "Off with her head!" I knew I had found my calling and pursued my studies with enthusiasm.

San Francisco State also had at that time the "Experimental College," a school within the larger school run by students. There were classes in all the disciplines with an emphasis on progressive and modern approaches to the material. Here I met Bill Kenney, a professor of education and a founder and teacher at Pinel, a small Summerhillian school in Contra Costa County. We read *Summerhill*. We discussed the ideas in the class in alternative education, sponsored by the Experimental College. The ideas were more freedom for the children—no strict disciplinary punishments. Bill told us how Pinel was similar yet different from Summerhill, the school in England. I was definitely gaining independence from Ron now, making friends and contacts that had nothing to do with our hippie life—connections that meant a lot to me. On the other hand, I was still deeply involved with Ron and our life and was not ready to change that.

Our Life and Times

Ron was charismatic. His height made him visible. His volubility assured him a place at the center of attention. Ron was well read in the contemporary Beat writers; he had taken many drugs; he had paid his dues in jail. He was 'hip.' He loved cars and motorcycles; he had a mechanical as well as an intellectual bent. He had a strong ego but did not push himself on people. He naturally dominated the conversation because he had a lot to say. At first I was overwhelmed by his personality, but I loved his sensitive side. He was my first lover, my first love. He taught me about my body, and because he thought I was beautiful, I stopped feeling inferior. When his mental illness broke through, I put up with it because it reminded me of home.

My dad was an alcoholic who abused my mother at times. As a young girl I remember loud arguments at night when I was in bed. Once my dad chased my mother down the hall of our apartment. She ran into the corridor of the apartment house. She endured the situation as all the neighborhood moms did. Most of the dads drank to excess, and we children knew very well the problems our families faced even if no one talked about these things. Alcohol, cigarettes, these habits were ubiquitous in the 1940s and 1950s.This was grown-up behavior.

Although the times and the family situation were different, there are strong parallels between the relationship mother and daddy and Ron and me. Both Mother and I were married to substance abusers: daddy to alcohol, Ron to drugs. Both of us were totally loyal to our spouses and tried to ameliorate the situation with positivity and love. In both cases, friends and neighbors were not involved. In fact, neither mother nor I sought consolation or assistance in dealing with the problems. We were close-lipped to the world.

* * *

We were getting very domesticated on Virginia Street in the Mission District of San Francisco in 1965. We had our cat, Sam, and then someone gave us two guinea pigs in a handmade cage with two levels connected by a ramp. Priscilla had short hair; John was a long-haired Peruvian. And their darling babies had cowlicks. The young were always a surprise since we were never aware that Priscilla was pregnant. Those cute juveniles appeared suddenly, miniature versions of adults, complete with eyes open, cheeping merrily for food. I was friends with neighborhood families, especially one family with three adolescent girls who were very helpful in finding homes for the newcomers. Our dear cat, Sam, was so mellow he allowed these rodents to walk across his belly as he lay on his back in the sun, drowsing.

Outside our back door was an unpaved road leading up Bernal Hill and passing the next and last house on our street. I had a recorder and sometimes at night I took it to the top of the hill where I sat in the bushes playing anonymously in the darkness. I even rented a piano. My mother had sent me my book of Beethoven sonatas to Tangier where I played in the practice rooms at a music conservatory. I treasured that book and now turned again to my favorite composer to satisfy my need to play.

In one of my San Francisco State College courses, we took a survey test to see what we really wanted as a career. The result for me was musician, way out in front of teacher, social worker and librarian. At that time I pooh-poohed that result thinking that was a fantasy. Now that I am a musician and have fulfilled my desire I think that was a damn good test.

One weekend morning Neal bounced up our steps and hammered on the door. The Grateful Dead were having a house warming party, and he was taking us to it. The Dead had bought a ranch in Novato, Rancho Olompali and that day they were celebrating. We were thrilled and got up immediately, dressed, and off we went. It was a beautiful June day, the sun shone and the bay sparkled as we followed Neal in our car over the San Raphael Bridge. At the ranch, the large colonial style white house was nestled in green rolling hills. The house had lovely hardwood floors, many rooms and no furniture to speak of, just a few tables and chairs. The happening was outside. We were there early in the afternoon and watched the party grow as the day progressed. There was a swimming pool but we had not brought suits and were not inclined to go in naked as many did. We got stoned on pot and hung out with Neal and others. The band was there but didn't play. It was a "Who's Who" kind of scene. Ken Kesey was probably there. Ousley was distributing his homemade acid. I did not partake that day and Ron demurred as well. We were out of our depth and we knew it.

As the sun was setting a buzz went around: Ali Akbar Khan, the great East Indian musician was about to arrive.

We rushed to the driveway just in time to see him step out of a car. He took one look around at this stoned out hippie scene and got back in the car and drove away. This was no place for a serious concert. Those of us in the driveway were disappointed, but we dispersed back to the lawn.

We had all read Ken Kesey's books and Neal told us stories of the bus trips across the country. Neal drove the "Merry Pranksters" bus. Now we were excited to learn of the Ken Kesey Acid Test coming to San Francisco in January 1966. The Kool-Aid at the event would be spiked with Lucy in the Sky with Diamonds and you could sample it or not. We had dinner at our house with friends and took our own tabs of acid afterwards. This time it was to be a fun hippie trip and not a spiritual experience.

The Fillmore Auditorium was alive and hopping with folks dancing and grooving under the strobe lights that seemed particularly intense that night due to our ingesting LSD. Neal was on the stage regaling us with stories in front of the Grateful Dead who were really cookin'. At one point the house lights went on revealing closed circuit TVs on the balcony focused on us dancing and cavorting on the main floor. Maybe this was supposed to be simulating Big Brother watching us, but no one around me was shocked, we expected the unexpected and we felt safe. At the end of the evening there was some kind of altercation with the authorities. Just a few people were left in the hall and Ron was about to challenge some pronouncement by the police, they had been called and were asserting themselves. I looked up to the balcony and saw Kesey standing, watching, he was not moving to do anything himself. I ran up to Ron and warned him not to be a patsy and get himself into trouble for something someone else had set up. He had second thoughts and sat down. Eventually we all left and no one we knew got into trouble.

There was meth-amphetamine around at this time and Ron started using it. I tried some too, by injection, remembering that Maxiton Fort in Tangier. The first time the meth felt similar, an intensely pleasurable physical and mental pulsation. The second time the thrill was not so strong. I recognized at once the addictive possibilities and decided that was the last time for me.

This type of hard drug activated Ron's paranoid schizophrenia, and he began moving away from me emotionally. His mood soured; he locked himself away in a shell. We didn't go to see friends or have friends over. One day I returned from school to find him sprawled out on the floor, a rifle by his side, and blood on his temple. Suicide? I knew he was in distress, but this didn't seem real. I knelt down and moved the gun away before I touched him and called his name. His eyes opened and he said, "The first thing you did was move the gun." He spoke in an accusatory tone like I had acted as if my safety was more important than his. He had set the whole scene up: taking some of his blood with a syringe and squirting it on his temple. I was very discouraged. He was sinking into despair and my positive energy was not helping. Later that evening he shot the rifle into the ceiling of our bedroom and I left the house.

I wandered through the neighborhood very distraught and frightened but stoic on the outside, like my mother. I ended up spending the night at an acquaintance's house a few blocks away. The people in the house did not ask any questions when I asked if I could spend the night. I slept in my clothes on top of the bed feeling homeless and despondent. Ron was not changing and I could not bring myself to leave him yet. Like a limpet in a tide pool I clung. The next day I screwed up my courage and went home. Ron was apologetic, he was very sorry to have frightened me. He said he needed a change. Why not go on a trip to Mexico? The semester was finishing and I agreed.

Mexico and Beyond, Late 1965

I was totally committed to my pursuit of an elementary teaching credential, but I had two weeks between semesters, and I agreed to go to Mexico with Ron. We spoke Spanish and loved the music and culture of that country. Maybe stepping away from our life in San Francisco would divert Ron from hard drugs. A new and beautiful landscape, and a different perspective might ease his pain.

We drove to the border, he sold the car in Mexico, and we hitchhiked to Guaymas and then Mazatlan. It was beautiful, the sun was strong and the flowers glowed with deep colors of red, yellow and blue. Ron was probably looking for drugs, but all he found was pot, happily for me. We roamed the marketplaces and towns, enjoying the villagy, less industrial environs. One night we splurged on an air-conditioned hotel to get some relief from the heat. We heard about a jungle town to the south, but thank heaven we didn't go there. That might have triggered an adverse reaction on Ron's tenuous psyche. The wildness of a jungle with no one around might have set off Ron's wild instincts to hurt himself and me. We hitched across the Sonoran desert with a lovely Mexican man and his two sons. We spoke some Spanish, he spoke some English, and we really liked each other. They took pictures of us. I felt a sense of normalcy in their presence. Ron was in a good mood in this familial atmosphere. Thus our Mexican trip ended on a happy note.

When we returned to our rented house on Virginia Street, in San Francisco, however, things had changed. Our neighbors had taken care of our pets, they were fine, but there had been a fire in the house across the street, and that house was destroyed. Ron's paranoia came to the fore again. Now he wanted to leave the city and visit his friends in San Luis Obispo. I was torn. I wanted to finish school, but I wasn't ready to give Ron up. I decided to take one semester off, which was allowed in the program, and give our marriage one last chance.

We gave our guinea pigs to neighbors and packed up the new used car with our few possessions and Sam, our cat. We had no cat carrier; we never thought of that. Sam rode in the front or back seat and seemed content once we got going. We must have let him out when we took a pit stop but he never ran away. He was our faithful familiar.

In San Luis Obispo, Alex and his wife and children welcomed us, and we stayed with them until we found a place of our own. Their house was a roomy ranch house with a lovely garden. I remember looking out the picture window in the living room and seeing Sam eat a bird he caught in the air.

We soon found a rental in Avila Beach just up the road a few miles. It was a charming old frame house set back from the street in that quiet beach town. The house was small and comfortable, and furnished. It was a five-minute walk to the seashore. I was reading Rachel Carson's book on tide-pools pursuant to the Nature Study class I had at San Francisco State. I would read a chapter on the animals in the tide-pools and then walk to the beach to see the real thing. The lovely sea snails and sea urchins in their purple garb, the hermit crabs scrabbling along in shells too big or too small, the limpets that clung tenaciously to the rocks as the tide washed over them. There were abalone too, on the larger rocks and at that time, it was not illegal to harvest them.

The hero of Ron's friends in this community was Ed Ricketts. He was an iconoclastic scientist of the sea. He left college after three years and set up his own research lab: Pacific Biological Laboratories on Cannery Row in the 1930s. He researched the sea life on the coast and wrote *Between Pacific Tides* with two other scientists. This book was the Bible of all interested parties: Alex and his friends. Many people had copies of this tome and it was passed around and discussed frequently. Ed Ricketts was very good friends with John Steinbeck; they were a pair of hard drinking, passionate men. In the early 1940s, after *Grapes of Wrath* was published and Steinbeck was besieged with positive and negative reactions, he and Ed took a boat trip to Southern California and Baha to research the sea life there. Together they wrote *The Sea of Cortez.*

Ricketts was an early ecologist, studying the tide pool animals as a community, emphasizing the relationships of animals and plants. Our friends were aware of the preciousness of sea life, and when they went diving for abalone they took a modest amount, what the community would use. They provided Ron with an extra wet suit and four or five people would go diving for the prized delicacy. They went in the afternoon, and later we gathered to help prepare the entrée. After the animal was removed from its shell the meat was pounded for a long time with a heavy wooden mallet. We all took turns at this arduous job. Then some seasoning and the provender was sautéed gently. I'd never tasted such delicious seafood. I still have several abalone shells from that time. They sit in my patio garden where their mother of pearl coating gleams in the sun.

One day Ron told me he wanted me to come with him to the shore while he would dive alone and explore an ocean cave. I sat on a rock holding a tether of some sort that was attached to his wet suit. It was a ridiculous situation. I never could have rescued him if he got into trouble, and we both knew that but we said nothing. The surf got rough and my rock was getting splattered with waves that were rising. Before I was totally engulfed I let go of the tether and moved back to the beach. Ron got out by himself and we were both discombobulated by this experience. Did he deliberately put me in a dangerous situation to test me? Was he testing himself to see how far he would go before drowning? It was a puzzlement. Neither one of us could verbalize these questions to seek answers. We both acted unconsciously. I went along with his crazy ideas as a loyal wife; he seemed bent on putting us both in perilous predicaments. Was he tempting fate?

One morning I woke up to see Ron standing over me with his hunting knife poised as if to stab me. I rolled over nonplussed but not fearful. That stopped him; he got into bed and touched me tenderly. "How do you feel?" he asked gently. "Numb," I replied decisively. Numbness had developed out of all these unresolved and perplexing situations and feelings. I wanted to pursue my interest in the science of the coastline, but I couldn't dislodge myself from this onerous relationship.

Our friends could see that Ron was a bit mad, but they never knew the extent of it. I was his intimate partner, and I had experienced his most irrational, indeed deranged behavior. I saw him in the depths of his despair and degradation. At that time I didn't see that that was very disturbing to him. No one wants an audience when the show is detestable. But Ron was not at the bottom below yet. He decided we would move again, to a dreadful little place near the roundhouse of a railroad yard—two shabby rooms with the constant clatter of trains switching back and forth. I didn't protest this move; I just followed along like an obsequious servant.

The night we moved in, Ron got very drunk and freaked out. He punched holes in the thin sheet rock walls. I was frightened. He was in a rage—over what, I couldn't figure it out. I tried to calm him down, but he threw me on the bed and forced himself on me. Rape. I was very distressed because of his actions, and because I had run out of birth control pills. The prescription was at a pharmacy in San Francisco. The possibility of becoming pregnant in these ominous conditions was overwhelming. I was desperate.

In the morning I sought a drugstore and a pharmacist who would sympathize with my plight and sell me a week's supply of birth control pills for five dollars, which was all the money I had. Fortune smiled on me and at the only drugstore in town, the pharmacist took pity on me. He could see I was almost frantic, though I was struggling to maintain my decorum. He kindly acquiesced to my request and sold me the pills for $5. I was grateful and relieved. I walked back to the railroad yard and sat on a rock in a desolate, hilly place. I felt demolished, humiliated, degraded. Putting my hand in my pocket I pulled out ten cents—one thin dime. I realized in that moment that this was Ron's trip, not mine. I liked to have enough money to support myself. This had to stop! I had to extricate myself from this hell.

That night I had another epiphany, an insight into myself that was distressing. I was looking at my face in the small, dingy mirror in the bleak, tiny bathroom. I saw dark circles around my eyes, the result of lack of sleep, stress, and anxiety. I also saw those dark lines as the makeup of a prostitute. I was prostituting myself, being untrue to my deep self, my higher self, my essence. Blindly following Ron through his traumas and suicidal inclinations was not what I was supposed to do. I had healthy interests and wanted to pursue life-affirming activities. I realized the extent of my degradation and vowed to find a way out.

The Beginning of the End

When I was working and going to college in San Francisco, I was involved in friendships with people who did not know Ron. Even though I never discussed my plight with these friends, they were an alternative to my miserable marriage. My mother was very gregarious and had lots of friends outside of her marriage, but she was loyal to my alcoholic father and did not discuss her predicament either. Even though I was a hippie woman supposedly liberated from convention, I felt the bond of marriage as strongly as my mother had.

However, breaks in the chain were appearing more and more. The realizations I had had in San Luis Obispo were causing me to doubt my tenacious hanging on to the withering and destructive relationship with Ron. I was clinging to someone who was going to pieces. When would I come to my senses?

Ron knew he was approaching rock bottom and although we never spoke of this, he too was looking for a way out. His solution to a bad situation was, as usual, to move on. He had news that his sister, Mia, was now living in Sausalito with her new husband, and they had extended an invitation to us to visit them. Once again, we packed up our meager possessions and our darling cat, Sam, who had stayed with Alex and his family for the past two months, and we hit the road north.

We arrived in Sausalito on December 30, 1966. Mia and her husband welcomed us warmly to their rental house nestled in the hillside above the main drag of the town. They invited us to stay in their guest room and made no objections to Sam. We must have looked harried and unhappy, but they never questioned us about that and we put up a good front. Ron was talkative; I was genial. Sam was beautiful with his long orange hair and his serene personality. We talked about our travels along the magnificent California coast, Ed Ricketts, abalone, the tide-pools, but of course nothing of Ron's aberrant behavior. He was still sinking; I could tell.

The next day, New Year's Eve, the four of us talked in the morning of going to a rock 'n roll club later to celebrate the new year. Then we all went our separate ways for a few hours. I walked around the lovely city by the San Francisco Bay. The houseboats were prominent and famous for the artists who called them home. It was a crisp, sunny day, and I was trying to gather myself together to move away. It was coming up on the time to enroll in the new semester at San Francisco State. I was looking forward to going back and finishing my teaching credential. I was not clear about how to do this. Would I tell Ron? Would I just disappear? I walked and I thought and drank in the Bay Area scene.

I got back to the house in the late afternoon and a crisis had developed. Ron was sitting on the bed in the guest room sharpening his hunting knife with a whetstone. He was silent and his eyes were glazed. He looked unapproachable. Mia pulled me over to the window in the door to the room, "Look at him," she said, "He's dangerous!" Mia was beside herself. She said he had been sitting there for hours, and she was thinking of calling the police. Her husband was anxious too, and said, "He's unstable; if anyone approaches him they will get hurt."

It was up to me. I didn't want the police involved, so I screwed up my courage and entered the room. I sat down beside Ron and saw that the knife had been worked on until it would split a hair it was so sharp. Ron was focused on the task and had a deranged gleam in his eyes. I was very frightened, but I suppressed that and acted like everything was normal. "Come on Ron, put the knife away," I said clearly and without emotion. "We'd all like to go to the club and dance; it's New Year's Eve. Mia and Don say it's a good band, and we all want to have fun tonight. It would be good to go out. We haven't been dancing for a long time." I continued in this manner without betraying the fear that was in the air.

As I sat next to him and watched him, I finally believed he wanted to kill me. He loved me, but he hated me, because I had witnessed his most degraded states of mind and body. I had helped him through difficult times and he appreciated that, but he also despised me for seeing how low he could go. He was conflicted about what to do. I kept up the sham that all was well, and if he put the knife away we would all go dancing and enjoy a New Year's Eve celebration. It finally worked. Without looking at me he put the knife in its case and we walked into the kitchen together.

The four of us kept up the dissembling that all was fine. We had dinner and went to the club. We smoked some pot in the car, and that put me in an out of body state. I watched myself dance with Ron under the strobe lights. It was like we were on another planet. "This is not real," I thought. I was still trembling inside and didn't feel that my feet were touching the floor. Ron acted affectionately towards me, thank goodness. Evidently his aberrations were in a separate part of his mind—he had forgotten the knife sharpening.

I don't remember getting back to Mia's place, but somehow I ended up sleeping by myself in the living room. When I woke up very early the next morning no one else was awake. I roused myself and decided to consult the I Ching. That book had been my companion for years, and I believed it had insight for me. I remembered when we were leaving Tangier; I got the hexagram "Splitting Apart." I wondered whether it meant leaving Tangier or leaving Ron. Now I knew I wanted to leave Ron and sought the advice of the Sage.

I threw my three Korean coins six times. The hexagram of Thunder over Thunder, "The Arousing," came up:

> Shock brings success
> Shock comes, "oh, oh"
> The shock terrifies for a hundred miles
> Thunder repeated: the image of SHOCK
> Thus in fear and trembling
> The Emperor sets his life in order
> And examines himself

> The line that particularly referred to me read:
> Shock comes bringing danger
> A hundred thousand times you lose your treasure
> And must climb the nine hills
> Do not go in pursuit of them
> After seven days you will get them back.

This was straightforward counsel. I was in Sausalito; the hills of San Francisco were a bus ride away. I threw a few things into a pillowcase and took off before anyone awoke.

The Unbearable Lightness of Being

I felt light and easy both in body and spirit, riding the bus from Sausalito to San Francisco that New Year's Day in 1967. At last I was carrying out my decision to leave Ron. A great burden had lifted. I wasn't celebrating yet, but I felt good—better than I had for years. I knew I was doing the right thing for me, and possibly for Ron too. My head was abuzz with plans. I would stay with Bob and Ellen our very good friends on Bernal Hill, but only for a few days. If Ron decided to track me down, that would be the first place he would investigate. I needed to go to San Francisco State College the next day to re-register and look for housing.

Ellen and Bob were very kind and sympathetic. They would put me up for a few days but definitely wanted to avoid Ron coming around to look for me.

The gods and goddesses were with me. Within a week I had a place to live in the Sunset District near San Francisco State. It was a commune of women: three bedrooms, two to a room. How comforting it was to be ensconced with five women, mostly students at the college in a well-organized home. Best of all was my roommate, Pauline. She and I hit it off immediately and to this day we are still friends. Pauline was finishing her high school credential in history. She was intellectual, witty, and compassionate. She empathized with my situation and supported me in my goal to become independent of Ron.

Back at San Francisco State, I enrolled in the courses necessary for my credential and to prepare me for student teaching in the fall. I renewed my student loan; things were going my way. I got involved with the Experimental College, a student organization that studied alternative learning methods and progressive ideas in general. There were classes in politics, sociology, the creative arts, and education. I signed up for the alternative education class.

It was exciting and intellectually stimulating to be back in school, on my own, and in a safe and nurturing environment. I must have been glowing in my happiness, because a friend of mine who played in a rock band wrote a song, "Sallie's Back." Indeed I was back at school, but more than that, I was back in spirit, back in action, back to my positive side. I wasn't home free yet, but I was stepping and dancing in that direction. I was freeing myself from an onerous relationship; I was becoming my true self, following my own inclinations, not someone else's. As I danced to the music at an event in the gym, I was thrilled. I knew the song was for me, even if few others did.

The Experimental College class in alternative education was sponsored and attended by Bill Kenney, a professor of education in the larger school. Bill was also one of the founders of Pinel School, modeled after Summerhill, the famous English School where classes were optional, and affirmation of the children was the rule. Pinel was in Contra Costa County, across the Bay from San Francisco. I had just read the book Summerhill and was excited to hear about Pinel, a school with a similar philosophy. Bill told us that at Pinel classes in the three Rs were required, but in the context of six acres of land and plenty of time to play, the classes were hardly a burden on the children. I was captivated by the description of the physical setting of the school, the open space and animals: goats, chickens, and a pony lived there. What an incredible contrast to urban public schools with their surrounding metal fencing, bells ringing to direct children to classes.

I resonated with the freedom the children were allowed in these progressive schools. They could choose activities, create projects, play outside with others or by themselves—all this in an atmosphere of safety and love. I was cutting the chains of a tired and destructive relationship; I was becoming free to be myself. While I was involved in my own liberation, these children had an opportunity to begin life in an unfettered, creative environment. I liked that. I was joyful in the anticipation of being with children in that kind of setting or, for that matter, in the public schools. I loved children. I craved their company. Their energy and vitality was drawing me to become a teacher.

The month of January 1967 was very full and satisfying. It started with the Human Be-in in Golden Gate Park. Friends and I got to the Polo Grounds early and sat close to the stage. Timothy Leary, Allen Ginsberg, and Gary Snyder were there, as well as the Grateful Dead and the Jefferson Airplane and other musicians. Women danced on the stage. We danced on the grass and marveled at the huge numbers of people who amassed there as the day went on. Colorful costumes, happy faces, hippie banners raised high, it was very comforting and exciting. Leary spoke of "tuning in, turning on and dropping out." Allen Ginsberg read poetry, chanted, and danced wildly. As the sun went down we were called on to face the sun and chant Sanskrit syllables. At the end Allen instructed us to turn around and pick up our trash. That thrilled me as much as the other events. We were respecting the earth and loving our mother!

I was inventing a new life. I took charge of myself; no more trailing around after Ron like a lost puppy. Nevertheless when Valentine's Day came around on February 14th, I found myself feeling sentimental. Despite my new perspective, I missed Ron and wanted to say hello to him. The abuse I had suffered and the sadness of seeing Ron deteriorate was not uppermost in my mind. The vitality and elán I was experiencing in my new pursuits replaced the dismal outlook of the last few years. I felt strong, so I called his sister's house. He answered after one ring. Was he waiting for me to call? We talked and I told him some of what I was doing. He told me that Mia, his sister, was about to give Sam away to a friend. "No," I said immediately,

"I'll come and get him."

I did, and I brought the dearly beloved feline to my new digs in the Sunset District. Happily my roommates loved Sam. There was no other pet at the house, and I really appreciated their openness. The I Ching prediction had come true. I regained my lost treasure.

In the process of retrieving Sam, I told Ron my address and he started to come by occasionally to see me. My roommates did not like him. He was not sociable, and he looked like a wraith—he was so thin and pale. Entering a well ordered, happy, female-saturated home such as ours, must have disoriented him. Undoubtedly, he was using some drugs that cancelled out any desire to socialize, if he had that desire anymore.

His purpose was to woo me back. I never engaged him in conversation about his past behavior. I was not ready for that conversation myself. I kept the talk as light and cheerful as I could. Once he asked if we could be alone in the bedroom. He gently but firmly made love to me orally; he knew I would climax that way. But orgasms be damned, my mind was made up. He could not entice me back.

On one of Ron's visits, my brother Fred was also there. Fred was a lieutenant in the Navy and was stationed at Yerba Buena for a short while. Fred said disapprovingly after Ron left, "He's just like Daddy!" Maybe Ron had been drinking, but he wasn't drunk, and yet Fred picked up a dependency, a weakness, and he was right. I didn't see that at the time, but later I saw the truth of that comparison.

Pauline and I went to a peace march that spring, one of the early protests against the Vietnam War. We marched behind Country Joe and the Fish and it was glorious. Another one of my involvements, political demonstrations that had been derailed by my marriage was revived. It was very satisfying and inspiring to be with hundreds of people and with Pauline, my buddy, feeling strong in our ability to make a difference. We felt powerful and wanted to change the world for the better. I felt that was possible. Wasn't I personally making a radical change for the good?

At an Experimental College workshop on alternative education, I met Ambrose Hollingsworth. He was an astrologer and a founder of a hippie commune called "Six Day School." The philosophy of this group was that the world was going through a major change and a new order of things was imminent. It was not a doomsday prediction. It was to ready ourselves for a new age that hopefully would be an age of brother/sisterhood: The Age of Aquarius. To that end the school would educate people in life, love, and wisdom, the foundations of the good life. There were classes in gardening, cooking, tools, pottery, meditation, dance, astrology, and tarot. Natural history of California, physics, and yoga classes were also offered. There was no charge for the classes, and a bus picked up people from the Bay Area to bring them to Glen Ellen in Sonoma County, the site of the school.

Ambrose liked what I said in the discussion at the workshop on the education of young children. We talked at length afterwards, and he asked me to come to the summer session of the school and be the caretaker of the young children. I liked Ambrose very much and the ideas of the school, but I wasn't sure if it was a cult or a clique of true believers. When I expressed my doubts, Ambrose said the only required belief was that essence precedes existence. I believed in the Great Spirit of the Native Americans, in the White Light of Tibetan Buddhism, and in the All That Is, so I agreed.

I joined the group in July, on the beautiful land in Glen Ellen, northern Sonoma County.

Six Day School Summer of Love 1967

It was a glorious hot, dry northern California summer day, and the caravan of cars meandered up the winding, seven-mile road to the Six Day School that had formerly been the "Top of the World Ranch." The fragrance of monkey flowers filled the warm air, pungent, befitting the landscape of green turning gold in the summer sun.

At the peak of the road, we drove by a large, muddy pond, a modern swimming pool and arrived at the parking lot by the main building, an ample, brown-shingled house. The house had many bedrooms, a spacious kitchen, and dining room, all in excellent condition and provided with comfortable, country décor. Across a nearby lush lawn, were three small cabins: Deer, Fox, and Raccoon. We were invited to choose a living space, either in the big house or a cabin. I chose Deer cabin, a one-room place nestled by a hillside and close to an outdoor bathroom—not an outhouse.

My dear kitty Sam and I settled into this charming abode. As time went on Sam would accompany me on walks around the hillside. His long, orange hair gleamed in the sunshine. I thought of him as my angel kitty—he never ran off, always seemed happy to be with me.

Leslie lived up the hill in a full-sized house with his attendant: he was a quadriplegic, the Co-founder of the school along with Ambrose Hollingsworth, my benefactor, who hired me to work at this paradise. Leslie and Ambrose had worked for different San Francisco rock bands. Both had been severely injured in car accidents. Ambrose was a paraplegic. They both used a wheelchair. They both used their insurance settlements to make the school/commune possible. Leslie and I became friends, and I can still see him in my mind's eye: his ebullient persona, his sparkling eyes as we discussed ideas and told each other stories of our lives. Ambrose lived in San Francisco and visited the school regularly.

I provided day care for the children of the parents who lived at the school and those who came up from the Bay Area to take classes. I loved my job. It was ideal for me and in this setting, idyllic. I gathered the children who lived on the land and the few who came with their parents on the bus, and every morning we headed for the pond. It was a Huckleberry Finn milieu: a muddy water hole with a homemade raft, croaking frogs, flying insects and birds sailing gently overhead.

Mud is perfect for young children—soft, gooey, dirty. It seemed to level things out between the younger and older children. Ours were three to eleven years old. Mud serves nicely as a remedy for bee stings: rub it on and it soothes the spot. Across the pond someone had erected a teepee to live in. One could imagine Native Americans in this environment. The air was warm and restful, and the quietude allowed us to listen to the buzzing and the chirping of the critters. We padded into the pond barefoot. Many of the children wore no clothes at all. They felt free and easy about that. We talked about the wildlife, sang songs, and generally lolled around until lunchtime.

The delicious meals, nutritious and plentiful, were worth waiting for. I needed plenty, because the diet was vegetarian. I had experimented with vegetarian diets before, but then I could always eat meat if I desired it. Here I had no choice. There was no meat, no chicken, and no fish. Without the nitty, gritty protein of animals,

The Pond — Six Day School 1967

I needed second helpings of everything! Thanks to the generosity of Ambrose and Leslie, second helpings were available. The kitchen opened every evening for snacks. I concocted a health food sundae: yogurt, cottage cheese, banana and honey.

The teachers and staff were friendly and outgoing to all. An inner circle of people formed the core of the school. They decided what was important and gave direction to the rest of us, but not much direction. Beyond the timetable of the classes and meals there were no strict rules, and no one was overseeing my handling of the children's daytime activities. I had no desire to be part of

Sallie by the Pond — Six Day School 1967

the inner circle; I relished cavorting with and providing activities for the children.

Those delightful young ones strolled along with me happily. In the afternoon, we had a covered area where we did art projects and I read and told stories. This was my first experience being in charge of a group of children ages three-to-eleven. I had no experience with three-year-olds and was unaware of their propensity to wander off if they were not directly involved in the activities at hand. One day while I was reading a story to the group, Sloopy, a three-year-old girl, wandered off. She fell in a ditch near the kitchen and her cries brought her mother, a cook, to the rescue. Sloopy had to go to the hospital for stitches. Her mother Mary, was very angry with me. I didn't learn of the accident till later in the day. Before Mary laid into me at dinner, other people told me it was not my fault, and I should not be intimidated by the tongue-lashing Mary had in store for me. I realized it was an accident and Mary was understandably distressed about her child, but I was not to blame for reading a story to the other children and missing Sloopy. After that, we had another person with me in the afternoon, and Mary kept her daughter with her.

There were lots of sweet, attractive young men at the school. One of them took a liking to me and he would whistle birdcalls outside my cabin in the evening. I knew what he wanted but I was not tempted. It would take many more months before I could relate to another man in an intimate way. I was still reeling from my overwhelming relationship with Ron.

When Ron and I married in London in 1962, I was very glad of it. I was thrilled by the romantic proposal and happy I could tell my parents and relieve their anxiety about me traveling around alone. They would have been horrified if they knew our situation: Ron using heroin and me helping him pursue a life of drug addiction. So, of course, I never told them the details of our life. Now that I was on my own, without Ron, I never had the thought that I was still married. Ron did not occupy my thoughts at all. I lived in the present and this present was blissful. In the midst of a beautiful natural setting, outdoors most of the day, working with children, surrounded by good people contributing their skills to educate others; nothing from the past touched me here.

I was not with Ron and I had no intention of ever returning to him. The fact that we were still officially married and that I still used his last name, never bothered me. What was a piece of paper in some office compared to what was happening in my life? I felt free, unencumbered by a husband who had abused me. I could live my life as I wanted to live it with no strings attached. I lived outside the grid, outside those official offices, and I intended to stay there. The counterculture suited me very well.

When I had time, I took a hike in the hills around the school, happy to be alone with nature. People smoked a little pot at night or on Sunday, our day off, but I felt no need to get high that way very much. The natural surroundings were seductive to me. I would lie face down on the dry earth and smell the air thick with heat and aromatic plants. The birdsong and insect chirps were music to my ears. A small stream burbled along, and I imagined my brain washed clean of past troubles. I was healing myself. I had no desire to stay at Six Day School beyond the summer. On the contrary, I was looking forward to returning to San Francisco State and student teaching. But this bucolic summer interval was therapeutic and cathartic for me. I realized that Ron did not want help from me nor the psychiatrist who offered him assistance. He preferred to wallow in the mire of his childhood traumas in a drug-induced state, sinking deeper into despair. This was not my way, I sought freedom from tribulation through doing good work, consorting with positive and happy people, and living the good life. I felt strong now, knowing I could continue my pursuits without worrying about someone else's problems.

Erlene and Philip were a couple that had a young

child, Ananda. Erlene was a beautiful African-American woman who taught classes in tarot. Philip, her handsome husband was a dark-haired, white man who taught astrology. The inner circle included Erlene and Philip. She was very poised and sure of herself and disciplined her daughter sternly in public at times. I surmised she regarded me as too lenient with my charges although she never said as much, and Ananda joined us sometimes. Not everyone had the same ideas about child rearing, but no confrontations occurred. It was summertime and the living was easy.

Marilyn had two children, a daughter eight years old and a son, six. Her son presented some adults with a challenge, but my approach was perfect for him. He could run and play in the pond, get muddy and mouth off about stuff as long as he didn't get physical with others. Marilyn's modus operandi was like mine, and we enjoyed each other. The six-day workweek did not permit a lot of time for hanging out and becoming intimate friends, but the connection between Marilyn and me felt good.

Another couple that lived near me had a dog named Collie. This female, part wolf, had puppies and kept them in the woods, away from people for a week or so. After that she allowed Nancy, her mistress, to accompany her to the litter-hiding place and meet the newborns. Nancy's partner Carl took a firm stand with Collie when she killed a chicken: she had to wear the carcass around her neck for a week to learn not to kill again. I saw the pain on Collie's face during that week and deemed that a harsh punishment. On the other hand, Collie never killed another chicken.

Sunday was the day off from working at the Six Day

Amanda and Sallie — 1967

School. No classes and no childcare for me. Often that was the day that rock musicians from San Francisco came to visit, namely the Quicksilver Messenger Service band members. They knew some of the inner circle at the school, and we all benefited from this friendship. We gathered on the deck outside the big house for impromptu rock concerts. The musicians played acoustic guitars and mostly without drums. This blended well with the quiet country setting and suited us very well.

One evening towards the end of the summer, I was sitting on the lawn with others waiting for dinner. As I gazed at the tableaux of green grass and Madrone forest surrounding us, two people emerged from the background and strode up to me: Ron and our good friend Bob. Ron looked unhealthy, thin as a rail, his tall frame stooping, his face grouchy. He looked like an old man at age 27. There I was obviously happy and relaxed with a whole group of hip, lively people in a lovely setting. I was free from his control, free from the dark cloud of our relationship. I smiled at him. "We're getting a divorce," he announced in an abrupt and irritated way. Then he turned and stalked off. Bob looked at me, puzzled, but turned and followed Ron. I was surprised at this encounter to say the least. I had had a passing thought to invite them to dinner, but I did not go after them. I accepted Ron's decision. It would be the right thing to get a divorce.

Ron had gone to some trouble to trace me to the school; maybe he wanted to get back together and control me again. It must have been a shock for him to see that I had made a new life. I had resources he lacked for starting anew. Too proud and angry with me for my success, he opted for separation, final separation, divorce. Ron nudged me to think about this, I saw he was right and decided that I would pursue the dissolution of our marriage.

Music Music Music

Music has always played an important part in my life. My parents were both musical, they didn't play instruments, but they sang. Dad's sister Janet, our closest relative in New York sang jazz on the radio, billed as "The Mississippi Miss." When she visited us, Janet accompanied herself on our upright piano. I remember her singing "in a quaint caravan there's a lady they call, the gypsy" in her lovely soprano voice. Mother sang in the Senior Choir at church and directed the Angel Choir, the young children. My two brothers and I sang in the choirs also. Dad sang lustily at the Christmas sing-alongs at our Brooklyn apartment.

I loved my piano lessons with Mr. Doxy, the kind, old gentleman who came to our place to teach me for years. He used the John Thompson Piano Books with pretty songs for beginners: "The Swan," "Lightly Row," "Country Gardens." As I progressed, there was a moody piece in a minor key that my dad liked. He would lie on the couch and ask me to play it again. At age seventeen I asked my mother for more rigorous lessons to learn Beethoven's music. She found Mr. Goldstein, and I studied Czerny and Beethoven piano sonatas. It was thrilling to me to play the Czerny exercises and the simpler Beethoven sonatas. I eventually got to the Pathetique and the Moonlight sonatas, and that was deeply satisfying. Beethoven's music penetrated my consciousness and reached a profound place.

I found it impossible to continue piano lessons when college academics took over my life, but I still played a little. I discovered the American Songbook pieces in several

Daddy, Mr. Faust, Aunt Janet, Mother, Bill, Katy, Sallie — Christmas 1956

books of show tunes and Broadway melodies. They were easy to read and resonated with my love of beautiful melodies: Time after Time, Lullaby of Broadway, Night and Day.

Reading over my journals of the '60s, I find the phrase: I need a piano, several times. Once when Ron and I were fairly stable in San Francisco, I rented a piano for several months. Mother had sent me my Beethoven sonata book, and I was happy to revisit the sonatas I had played before.

I danced through my life too: Retta's Dancing School for tap at six years old, the Lindy, and the Foxtrot with my friends as a teenager. In San Francisco in the '60s, we did free-style hippie dancing to the San Francisco bands: The Jefferson Airplane, The Grateful Dead, The Quicksilver Messenger Service, Janis Joplin and Big Brother and the Holding Company. I can still see Janis on stage, sweating, giving her all, belting out her heartfelt blues. Janis embodied one woman's soul, her plight, joyous yet unfulfilled, lamenting, wailing her songs. For me, stoned on pot or tripping on LSD, dancing under the strobe lights at the Fillmore was consummate.

On my own, after the break with Ron, I continued to go to the dances at the Fillmore, the Carousel Ballroom, The Family Dog place on the beach-front, the Avalon Ballroom. I loved the Grateful Dead, never a "deadhead" per se, but I loved dancing to their music. It was hypnotic to me, and I was transported to a lovely place moving to Jerry Garcia's guitar solos. One night at the Carousel I saw Jerry coming towards me on the dance floor after the set finished. He was a stocky man with unkempt dark hair and beard. His plaid shirt was casually falling over his jeans. I stopped him and told him how much I liked his music, how it moved me to dance my feelings. He pooh-poohed my compliment, saying something like "It's just music," in a disparaging way. I was not abashed or put-off, although I was surprised at his dour attitude.

Another night at the Carousel Ballroom I went to see Chuck Berry. We danced up a sweat and got high on the music we had heard since we were young teens. On the break I went over to the concessions area to get a drink, and there he was: Chuck Berry drinking a soda and talking to people. He was tall, lean, muscular. His face radiated energy and well-being. I waited my turn and then told him how much his music turned me on. "It's so upbeat and joyous, it makes me happy, and I dance to express my delight!" He was receptive to my enthusiasm and smiled. Then he asked for my phone number! I laughed and said it wasn't like that. "Okay," he replied undeterred, "Here's my number if you change your mind." He wrote his number on a matchbook, and I put it carefully in the back pocket of my jeans. I kept it for a while with no intention of calling, just to remember his geniality.

That spring I had a boyfriend, Gerhard. He was a liberal German immigrant I met hitch-hiking. He was a Taurus like me, and we had some wild and sensuous times together at Big Sur taking LSD. This is from my journal at the time:

Sunday acid on Big Sur mountain early in the morning
turn on and watch and warm in the golden sun
frolic naked on the road and flee to a secluded spot as day

moves on
It's a psychedelic picnic the psychedelic snake has wrapped his bright orange body around the high mountain the first day of Taurus my love's birthday is sunny and breezy and the mountains move with the wind
He stands like a lion on the hillside surveying his realm
His prey at his feet
I feel playful and we laugh and laugh
it's good we play and laugh and make love
in the
sunshine slowly we climb to the top finding better, more beautiful, warmer, more
comfortable places as we go up

Gerhard and I went to several anti-Vietnam War marches together. With his long hair and colorful headband, he fit right in. But this affair was "too hot not to cool down" as the song says and a few days or a week later all was changed. I hadn't heard from Gerhard for some time. We had been so passionate and wanting to see each other a lot; I was wondering what had happened. He had left some hits of acid in our refrigerator in the women's commune where I lived on Bernal Hill. He had left a pair of jeans in my room. Finally he called. He wanted to come by and pick up his LSD. "Fine," I said. I rolled up the jeans to hold in my right hand behind the door I opened with my left. I was reluctant to return his clothes, thinking I would see him again. When I passed him the acid, I noticed a movement behind him. It was a girl, obviously his partner for the acid trip. This made me mad. I threw the jeans at him and slammed the door.

Jealousy was not my favorite emotion, but there it was, I expressed my wrath. Later I heard from one of my roommates that he was "afraid" of me. To me it was funny and empowering that anyone would be afraid of me.

Whenever a relationship with a lover ended, I didn't feel lonely. I was glad to have time alone and integrate the experience. I had friends and my life was changing and developing in the best way. I didn't miss the sex. It was sweet with Gerhard, but I wasn't in love with him.

I was twenty-eight now, and I realized I had been smoking tobacco for ten years. Time to stop. I was rolling cigarettes using "Bugler" tobacco bought in a can. Rolling engaged the hands and took a little time so that helped cut down smoking. I decided that would be the last can of tobacco, so that slowed me down to make it last. Finally there was no more tobacco. I bought a bunch of sesame-honey crackers at the health food store, and when I craved a smoke, I put one of those crackers in my mouth. They were very sticky and gooey. My tongue started working to remove the stuff from between my teeth. This was my invention and it worked for me! In two weeks, I had no more cravings. It was also the right time for me since I was pursuing my dream of teaching young children, and that was very satisfying.

The music in my life then was the Beatles "Sergeant Pepper's Lonely Hearts Club Band" and Bob Dylan. I'd put on the album "Blonde on Blond," a two record Dylan album and stand the covers up on a chair, so I had a complete picture of him. I danced to Bob; he was my faithful guy. I was in love with his music.

Becoming Independent

The housing service at San Francisco State College was very useful. I found another house rented by women students on Bernal Hill. Sam and I secured a room in this house. No one else had a pet and they were all taken with mine. He was beautiful to look at and easy to get along with. I had lived on a different side of Bernal Hill with Ron. Both sides had the best weather in San Francisco. When it was overcast and rainy in the Sunset District, where SF State was located, it was sunny on Bernal Hill. Both times I lived there, my house was close to the top of the hill. It was lovely to walk in the sun with wild flowers blooming, and it was safe at night for moonlight strolls.

At the college, I registered for student teaching and the Experimental College. It was exciting. I renewed old friendships and met new people. I was glowing with the great joy I felt in pursuing my own interests, in being on my own, liberated from Ron. A great onus had been lifted, and I felt buoyant and thrilled at the prospect of each new day.

My interest in men beyond friendship was kindled by Paul, a handsome photographer I met. We had many common interests: music, art, desiring freedom from conventional ways of being, probing our inner-selves to discover who we were under the veneer of our backgrounds. We had both taken LSD and had no desire to trip again but treasured the memory of those experiences. We had learned that not all is as it seems to be: there are layers of existence and meaning below the everyday work-eat-play-sleep world. We both wanted to know more of the deeper selves that pop up in dreams and drug experiences.

Paul would muse: "Photographs are more than pictures of a face or a scene. Good photographs suggest that under the surface there are more profound emotions and dimensions. Photographs can have deep political and social significance like Dorothea Lange's images of the dust bowl people in the thirties."

I remembered: "When I took acid at Big Sur, I would hug trees and blink my eyes to see the world as usual and then blink again and see the trees, plants, animals and people with psychedelic colored edges and an iridescent quality that made everything other-worldly. I buried my underpants in the sand to symbolize stripping away the outer garments to discover the naked truth."

Paul and I went camping one weekend and he initiated me back into the pleasures of making love. We felt a kinship and a closeness, but we were not "in love." Sex could be part of a relationship between two people, but it did not necessarily mean a lasting relationship. Sex was not casual; it was significant, but not binding. What an expansion of consciousness! We could include physical intimacy in a friendship without tying knots around the people involved. Paul and I had an understanding of this concept. We enjoyed the intimacy, but we both had self-development and careers as our primary focus. We continued our relationship for many months. Paul took a series of photographs of my fifth grade class and me in the Mission District in the spring. You could see from these photos how much I loved teaching and how much the children were enjoying my projects. One black girl was peeking at the pictures in the book: *The Family of Man*. I brought that book in for the children. The regular teacher was lecturing, droning on about dates and places, while the girl was sneaking a look at pictures of families around the world.

At the Experimental College, I signed up for a program called "Each One Teach One," a one on one tutorial service for disadvantaged children who needed remedial help. I was assigned a Latina girl about nine or ten years of age. We became close over the course of our tutorials. I was very happy to help her with the basic skills of reading and writing. About six months later, when she and her family moved out of San Francisco, she wrote me a letter. Her charming scrawl expressed her feelings: "Dear Mrs. Hardage, I like you very much. You help me with my work and I feel better. I miss you here my address, cum see me." I was very touched.

The tutors in the program had regular meetings to discuss our assignments and the political and social impact of the program. These discussions were often heated. The black tutors were becoming more radical and questioned whether the white tutors should be with black children. The conversation was animated. "It is not fair to black kids to build trust in white people; they will not be prepared to deal with racism."

"The white man always betrays the black man."

"Wait a minute, here we are black and white together with common goals, the education of children."

"Black people are in a different situation. They deal with racial slurs and discrimination all the time."

"Can't we show by example that it is possible for all of us to get along?"

"Black children must be wary; they can't expect to be treated equally."

"White people cannot be trusted."

This all came to a head when a black child from this program was brutally kicked by a white man. The young boy was walking in a park near his home with his sister and saw a man he thought was his tutor. The white man was tall, with dark, short hair and was wearing jeans and a jean jacket as his tutor often wore. The boy ran happily up to this man and swung himself around on the man's leg, a game he played with his tutor, but this time with disastrous results. This incident was the proof the radical black students needed. It was decided that the integrated approach was not working for black children, and there would be no more mixed race tutor-tutee. I thought this incident, the boy being kicked was deplorable, but it was the exception, not the rule. Nonetheless I did not protest the decision.

Also at the Experimental College I met Oscar, a very sweet and talented African-American filmmaker. He had made a short film: "A Bridge Tomorrow," that I found very relevant to the times. In the film two boys, one black, one white, are playing at the beach. They are attempting to build a bridge across a stream of water. The bridge keeps collapsing and they try again. Finally, they give up. One boy puts his arm around the other and says: "We'll build a bridge tomorrow." The film was beautifully done and very meaningful to me. I asked Oscar if I could show it to my first grade class. He agreed to lend me his only copy with the admonition to take very good care of it. I promised. After I showed the film to my class and discussed the ideas with the children, I told a fellow student teacher at the same school. He asked if he could borrow it and show it to his class that afternoon. I foolishly agreed and gave it to him assuming he knew how to run the projector properly. He didn't and tore the leader section of the film, the lead in before the film started. Even though the tear was not on the film proper, I was devastated. Oscar was very upset and that ended our budding friendship. He berated me righteously and rightfully for allowing someone else to use his film; he had not approved that. I felt terrible for a long time about the damage to the film and very sad about losing Oscar as a friend.

The first grade class was my first student teacher assignment, and after watching the teacher and participating a little, I took over the class. The regular teacher withdrew. It was difficult for me to keep the children's attention. I was very green, and the kids could tell I was not a strict disciplinarian. They talked to each other during the lesson and got up to walk around. One day they were particularly uncontrollable, and all my ideas and procedures were useless. The kids were loud and disruptive and almost in an uproar. I was at my wit's end and stepped out of the classroom to gather myself together. I was at sea. It was lucky for me no one saw this given that it was not the recommended thing to do. Fortunately, when I came back into the classroom after a few minutes, the children had calmed down. Another class might have demolished the room under those circumstances. Eventually I developed a rapport and some control over this group and ended up enjoying it.

Meanwhile Six Day School, where I had spent the summer, was still in operation and I found ways to visit. (It would be years before I learned to drive.) I was surprised at the change in the psychological climate of the place. The inner circle had tightened their control over the teachers and staff. There were more rules and regulations and more philosophical tenets to believe in. I felt sorry about this. It presaged the demise of the school. I enjoyed visiting the land and my friends who still lived there. One night I went for a walk with Blair, a musician friend. The sky was crowded with stars and planets, but no moon; it was dark. I walked into the branch of a pear tree, knocked out my contact lens, and scraped my cornea. It was very painful, feeling like I had a piece of glass in my eye that I couldn't get out. We couldn't go to the hospital in town until the next morning, so it was a sleepless uncomfortable night for me.

The next morning the doctor at the emergency room patched my eye and said it would heal itself. I was to keep it covered. The pain eased as it healed, and I bought a black eye patch to follow the doctor's orders. Back at San Francisco State, it was Halloween and people were celebrating. I dressed in a bright orange blouse, black skirt and the patch. Bill Kenney, our alternative education teacher in the Experimental College, saw me in the hall in that get-up and for years afterwards told the story of me in that colorful, flamboyant costume. He was impressed.

Bill and I were becoming good friends. I was drawn to Bill's ideas, experience, and charisma. He was a talker, soft-spoken but loquacious, and articulate. Bill was empathetic and a good listener. He was happily married to Alice, with three children, and later I became a friend of the family. Bill was a college professor, but his life centered on his family and Pinel School, the Summerhillian School he helped to found. All his children went to Pinel, as did the children of the other founders. "We test the waters with our own offspring," Bill would say. It was indeed a test of their beliefs, for many of the founders' kids played outside for years before learning to read and write. For middle-class white people, this must have been trying, but the theory was correct. When the children learned their basic skills, they excelled. Bill was the mentor I needed, a father figure with expertise and experience in my chosen field. A sensitive man, he never pushed his point of view on a person; rather, he made the ideas so appealing and meaningful you could not resist them.

My circle of friends and colleagues was widening. More and more people were coming into my life. This filled any void I might have had when I left Ron. My ideas about being an independent woman were being realized. The connections I made were all healthy and positive. I didn't miss Ron and our life together at all. I had invented a new, more constructive existence. Life now unfolded in ways that made me feel a part of a greater whole. That was very satisfying.

1968 The Times They Are A-Changin'

The year began quietly and gently for me, a far cry from the dramatic New Year's events at Ron's sister's house the year before. This time I went to a party at Ellen's house in Corte Madera. Ellen and Bob had been very close friends when I was with Ron, and they sheltered me when I fled from him on New Year's Day 1967. Ellen had since left Bob and was living with her young son in Marin County. At the party, we ate and drank with good company. The atmosphere was low-key and decorous rock music played softly in the background. I came with Pat, a friend to Ellen and me, who lived in Berkeley. We left before midnight and on the drive through the Marin neighborhood to the freeway, we talked about the changes that were happening to us. I had split from Ron, Ellen had separated from Bob, and Pat's husband was in China for his work. Pat was at home with the responsibility of their two young children. Suddenly as we drove we heard raucous noise from the street: yelling, carousing, the clattering of pots and pans. The New Year had arrived.

From time to time I would hear about Ron from mutual friends. It was not good news. Either he was in jail or at Napa State Hospital for acting out. At first I was surprised, I thought he would pull himself together as I was doing. To me he had been the bedrock of our marriage. He taught me about sex, about keeping a house in order, about being on the cutting edge of the counterculture in literature and music. Now I realized, he had been leaning on me for stability. I knew how to get a job, to work, and make money apart from family inheritances. I could follow a schedule and get things done in

Hippie Girl — 1968

the everyday workaday world. I didn't need substances to accomplish this. I liked smoking pot with friends, but my energy was directed towards improving my life and furthering my career as a teacher.

I was on my way to becoming my own person. My life was coalescing; Ron's life was unraveling. I felt sad that he was falling apart, but I had no desire to help him anymore. All my dedication when I was with him did nothing for him, and now he struggled alone. I needed to extricate myself further. I found out about Legal Aid, and what I needed to do to get formally divorced. The whole procedure would take many more months, but I got started.

My second student teaching assignment was a fifth grade class at a school in the Mission District. The children were mostly black and brown. The regular teacher was a white woman with a totally traditional, boring approach. She read out of a history book with dry dates and facts, and the children sat there uninterested. They were very well behaved kids and didn't act out obstructively in the classroom. Gradually I took over the teaching duties. I felt more at ease with these older children and once the regular teacher had withdrawn, I did more daring lessons with them. For a social studies lesson, we moved the desks and chairs around and set up a peace conference between the North and South Vietnamese groups and the Americans. These ten-to-eleven-year-old children knew a lot about the war and enjoyed bantering various issues in their assigned roles.

Once, I did a relaxation meditation with this class. They sat at their desks with a sheet of paper and pencil, and I asked them to close their eyes as I guided them to relax their bodies. "Take a deep breath and wiggle your toes gently, then relax each toe, one at a time. Take another deep breath and relax your legs, let them feel heavy on the floor." After traveling up to the head, relaxing each part, I had them open their eyes and draw a self-portrait on the sheet of paper. The results were amazing. Many of the kids disparaged themselves, drawing squiggly lines indicating bad odors, arrows pointing to ugly faces, or fat bodies. Others were ecstatic pictures of themselves as hippies in wild costumes. I felt very good about this experience. The class was more than willing to do this very personal and intimate digging into their inner selves.

Another day we moved the desks and tables off to the side to make a big dance floor. I put on the sound track of Zorba the Greek, and we danced in a line like the traditional Greek dancing, and then broke away and did our own interpretive dance. Not everyone was uninhibited enough to join, but everyone enjoyed the music.

When I left this class at the end of the semester and the regular teacher came back, I got many good-bye cards, some with pictures of tears flowing! They complimented me and said how much they would miss me and implored me to come back to visit them. What a beautiful and rewarding experience for me.

Still active in the Experimental College, I was fascinated by the Esalen Institute in Big Sur, California. The human potential movement took experiments with LSD and other drugs seriously. Meditation, Eastern religions, and philosophy as well as Gestalt Psychology were explored. One of my friends knew Michael Murphy, the director of Esalen, and Michael offered my friend the use of his rooms at Esalen over a weekend when he would be away. My friend and I hitchhiked to Big Sur along the spectacular coastline where Esalen was located. We were allowed on the grounds to wander and use the hot baths but not to participate in workshops, as we were guests.

What a treat! It was early spring, the lovely grounds were lush with grasses and some flowers. The air was cool, but the sun shone on the Pacific Ocean and the water gleamed with rainbow colors. We haunted the hot baths at night. These natural springs were perched on a cliff overlooking the ocean. As we soaked our naked bodies we imbibed the moonlight reflected on the sea, sparkling and magical. The multitudinous stars glittered and shimmered in the waves. We slept on the floor of Michael's apartment in our sleeping bags. We were friends, not lovers, and we enjoyed ourselves very much.

Gestalt Psychology was in the forefront of new therapeutic approaches. The emphasis was being in the present moment, not escaping into the past or the future. To gain maturity, to stand on your own two feet, so to speak, and to regain lost potential were the goals. Fritz Perls was the guru of this movement in 1968, and I liked his description of the three levels of the mind: the first, is the phony personality we present to the world that covers the second level of emptiness and fear, that covers the third level that is the real stuff of ourselves that connects to the collective unconsciousness of all people. This last level is our dynamic personality that is free and relaxed and can explore new ways of being and communicating with others.

The Experimental College invited Perls to come and do a workshop at San Francisco State College. I was assigned the duty of meeting him at the parking lot and escorting him to the workshop venue, a small one-room building in the midst of larger campus buildings. I knew what Perls looked like from photographs, an older man (seventy-five), medium height, with grey, unruly hair, and glasses. I greeted him and we walked to the workshop together. I was not a participant since I had not paid the fee. I stood in the back of the room and observed.

He designated the chair for the therapeutee as the "hot seat," and those brave enough to sit in it would respond to Perls's questionings. He had his following, indeed some worshipped him uncritically. The room was full and the excitement was palpable.

As I watched and listened, I felt Perls's method of cracking the first two levels of the mind to get to the third was harsh. He showed no mercy when asking questions to the person in the hot seat and called attention to their nervous habits.

"Do you have stage-fright?"

"You are covering your chest, why?"

"You are swinging your legs."

"That's just an excuse."

"Are you a little girl?"

"You're a phony."

"You're bluffing."

One young man broke down in tears. It seemed to me that Perls was too hard-edged, like a strict father figure trying to break a person's spirit rather than open them up to possibilities. Granted, I only viewed the one workshop; maybe he was having a hard day.

After the workshop I took Perls to the Experimental College office where we confabulated with other staff people, and Perls led a mini-workshop for us. At one point he said, "We all come to the wailing wall and release our troubles." I countered with, "Some of us come to have a 'whale' of a good time!" He liked that, we all laughed and released the tension we felt between the guru and us. I was not in awe of him and he knew that. I walked him back to his car and, to my surprise and dismay, he invited me to come back with him to his hotel. I was shocked inside, but laughed and said, "No, I have other commitments."

What shocked me was that he, a man forty-six-years-older than I, and supposedly in possession of great wisdom, was ready at a moment's notice to go to bed with a stranger. This was a bit hypocritical of me, for in hindsight, I know I too was ready to make love with someone I was attracted to, possibly a stranger. Somehow I thought a "guru" was beyond that. Not so.

I never would have had these experiences if I had stayed with Ron. Our life was so narrow at the end. We were consumed with our problems and ourselves. Now my world was widening and deepening, and I was growing inside to embrace a larger universe. It was time to officially cut the tie that had bound me. In 1968 you could not get a divorce on the grounds of incompatibility. You had to prove abuse, mistreatment, or adultery. I asked Ellen to testify with me that Ron had abused me and physically hurt me. She agreed. What a dear friend; she had never witnessed the mistreatment, but she knew it had happened, and she supported my plea. The Legal Aid lawyer set up a court date, and after our testimony, the judge granted me the divorce immediately. He asked me, "Would you like to use your maiden name again?" I had not even thought of this, but said, "Yes, thank you," at once. I was grateful to Ellen, the judge, and the state of California for releasing me from a very bad marriage. It cost me $35.

BERKELEY

1968 A Momentous Year

In April of 1968, Martin Luther King's assassination shocked the world. I found these words in my journal of that time. (Please note: the word "cat" is beat/hippie lingo for "man.") The kids throwing rocks in this piece were playing, not attacking anyone.

4/6 Aftermath of MLK's assassination
A memorial at noon on campus.....thousands silent and heads bowed in prayer
Revolutionary black students demand revenge - kill, kill, kill
This fits the historical reality of our times it is momentary justice
In hippie homes the pipe is passed and the scene goes on uninterrupted
Seduction, music, stoned conversation
Outside Buena Vista Park is quiet and beautiful trees logs children
Haight is electric with people black and white together
Those who have transcended
On the corner a dog is run over and hurt he yelps
We run to see and help his leg is skinned and bleeding
Big Indian cat lifts him and brings him to his truck we wait for SPCA
Beautiful Indian caring for his dog
People do care People do get involved People do love
A kiss is blown to me from a black cat in a car - turns abruptly away like he's not

Supposed to do that
Kids throwing rocks *'hello you pretty honky'*
The I-Thou coffee house scene is eternal: stolid, safe, intellectual conversation

When I wrote this in 1968, I was aware of the contrasts of assassination and hate versus caring for people, animals, and love. Indeed, that was the essence of my awareness: the two conflicting sides of human nature, the will to care, the will to do harm. In those tumultuous times of the 60s, one could find many examples of those two sides in public and private life. In San Francisco, the general public was appalled by the assassination. The thousands that grieved were both black and white. The radical black students were a small but vocal minority. Even strangers were telling me they wanted to be in a world where love triumphed over racism and hate. I was about to find that world.

In May, my friend Bill Kenney, college professor and teacher at Pinel School, asked if he could come over to my place; he had an important question to ask me. "Of course," I replied, intrigued by what the question could be.

Bill told me that his wife, Alice, a teacher at Pinel wanted to take some time off from working and his question was: "Would you like to take her job and be in charge of the young children at Pinel?"

"Yes, I would like that very much," I answered. I was thrilled!

"The salary is low," Bill informed me, "Quite a bit lower than public school, but you would be covered by Kaiser, our health plan."

"Sounds good to me."

"Please take some time to think about this and we'll talk later."

After Bill left I thought about the offer for about an hour, then called him at his home. "Yes, yes, I definitely want to teach at Pinel, thank you for the opportunity." We were all happy. It was my dream come true.

Now that I had a job in Contra Costa County, across the Bay from San Francisco, I needed to move to the East Bay. Berkeley would be ideal for me, a city known for its political and intellectual aspects. I investigated housing and summer jobs. Newspapers had classified ads offering these services. There were mainstream newspapers and counterculture ones. In San Francisco we had *The Good Times* and *The Oracle* as counterculture papers. *The Berkeley Barb* was prominent in the East Bay. The Berkeley Co-op supermarket had a bulletin board bulging with index cards.

I found a communal living situation on College Avenue and a summer job at Camp Kitov, attached to a synagogue. Perfect. I learned the Jewish songs teachers sang on the bus on the way to Tilden Park, where the activities were set up. The house on College Avenue was populated with theater people, who were very active in their field. I participated in a comedic film made in the house while I was there. But the traffic on College Avenue was oppressive to me and my kitty, Sam. I couldn't let him outside. After a month I looked again and found another lovely, old Victorian house with young people renting rooms on Ocean View Drive, two blocks above the busy College Avenue. Sam and I moved in.

The first adventure at Pinel School was a camping trip. The school year began and ended with the whole school, teachers, students, and some parents, bundling ourselves and our supplies into a big, yellow school bus and a few cars, driving off to the Sierras for four days. Some brought tents, and some, like me, slept under the stars.

As the young children's teacher, I staked out a campsite close to the campfire for the little ones and me. After the wonderful songs that were sung around the campfire led by Jim Stein and his guitar, the ghost stories began. Oops, I quickly gathered my tribe and whisked them away to our nest nearby. We were close but out of hearing range. After tucking each one into her/his sleeping bag, I regaled them with fairy stories and folk tales I embellished and edited for their nighttime pleasure. I wanted no scary dreams, no screams in the night. It worked very well for them and me.

The three male teachers, Bill, Ray, and Jim, took turns cooking the evening meal, and each one had his own cooking style. Ray was noted for his herbal additions; dill weed was a notorious flavor connected to Ray. On one camping trip after we finished a Ray dinner, we were sitting around talking at the picnic tables. We became aware of a chanting sound coming from the surrounding trees. Into the eating area came a procession of down-in-the-mouth children moaning: "We died of Ray's cooking. We died of Ray's cooking." The procession proceeded to the center of the space and one-by-one the children fell down in a heap, done in by dill weed. Ray rose to the occasion and with grand gestures and Latin gibberish, he performed the last rites—an unforgettable scene.

* * *

The house on Ocean View Drive was very comfortable and the company was pleasant. But I began to realize that I wanted my own kitchen. No one was particularly messy, it was just that I wanted to do things my way every day. So once again, I started to look for another place to live, my own place this time—at age twenty-nine, I was more than ready. One Saturday afternoon, I went to the Berkeley Co-op to check their bulletin board. There it was on a card: studio apartment near the Co-op, $80 a month including utilities. I must have known that was it for me, because I took the card itself rather than writing down the information. I walked a few blocks to Deakin and Prince streets. The house was right on the corner, a lovely old Victorian painted white, weathered, and looking friendly. It had round windows on the first and second floor right at the corner; it looked like a ship setting out on a calm sea. The owner Mr. Palmer, a gracious African-American man, showed me the second story, small flat. A long hall led past the bathroom, the kitchen, and ended in the living room. There were windows on the south and west making the space warm and light. Yes, this was it. I took out forty dollars I had in my pocket, for a fall sweater I was planning to buy, and I paid half the rent in advance.

I didn't know anyone in Berkeley yet, so my dear fellow teachers and older students helped me move in. We painted the living room ceiling and one wall purple, the rest white. The kitchen became bright orange with deep blue cabinets and refrigerator. I was in heaven. Sam had a rooftop place outside the living room window where he jumped to the next roof and down into the yard. I realized I wanted to change Sam's name. He was a very special being and needed a more appropriate appellation. His orange color reminded me of my orange-Irish background. I had been reading a book by Krishna Murti and came up with "Krishna Murphy" for Sam's new name. I started a friendship with a Pinel parent, Tigger. We explored the nightlife of Berkeley, dancing at the Long Branch or having a beer at the Starry Plough. I was settling in nicely.

One sunny, warm day in October, I was dancing at Provo Park (now Martin Luther King, Jr. Park) to a rock band with some friends. I was very happy, barefoot, and carefree. At the end of the song, I looked over at the band. There was Ron hanging around the drums, smiling at the drummers, but looking absurd in a wool topcoat on this warm day. I sped out of there without saying good-bye to anyone, without my shoes. I ran home, a mile or so in my bare feet propelled by the desire to be out of sight. Ah, my new abode was my hideaway; he would never find me. He never did. I did receive a letter via my Legal Aid divorce lawyer. It was a poem of regret and resignation. I barely read it but immediately called the lawyer to say, "No more communications, ever!" He complied. "Amen."

Pinel School 1968

It was a joy to work at Pinel, located on six acres of hilly land in Martinez, east of Berkeley. The classrooms and other buildings: library, assembly room, known as the 'Big Room,' and bathrooms were detached from each other—1950s-style, ranch-type affairs. They were spread over the lower part of the land. The Tower, a climbing structure for play, was situated on the highest part of the land. We had a carpool for the Berkeley kids and me. When BART was built in 1970, we had a school bus pick us up at the Lafayette station. The air was fresh, the sun was bright, and the rains were monsoons in those days. In the rainy, winter weather season the children did mud sliding. They used cardboard on the big hill and slid down raucously. On the smaller hill outside my classroom you slid into the creek. When I tried sliding, it was exhilarating, and the creek water was warm and gooey, a truly primal experience. One had to bring extra clothes to do mud sliding. I put down butcher paper on my classroom floor for the shivering sliders to dry off and warm up near the heater.

The children were active outside playing. Some of the older children, mostly boys, built forts from scrap wood they found on the grounds or brought from home. The boys, ten to twelve years old, sneaked prohibited tobacco and marijuana cigarettes into their makeshift hideouts. We spent a lot of time discussing this situation at the weekly teachers' meetings. At one point we told the kids they needed parental approval of smoking, and they needed to police themselves so that only the ones with permission smoked and no young children were

Pissbeard — Pinel 1969

allowed in. Many of the children at Pinel had parents who were divorced or separated and often were recovering from bad home and school experiences. We teachers felt these children needed private places to escape from the tensions of their lives.

The older boys were a problem for me at first. They were often vitriolic in their language, swearing at me and the younger children. I was very assertive in my defense of the little kids when they were bullied. This earned me the "Militant Mother Award." I didn't proscribe the swearing at me personally, thinking that I would alienate these boys. I needed to figure out how to become friends with them. I did challenge them sometimes. One time, I needed to rototill a patch of land I had fenced off for a vegetable garden. I teased those big boys saying:

Sarah, Diedra with flowers — Pinel 1970

"This is probably too hard for you guys. The rototiller is heavy and you probably couldn't handle it." That got their dander up; they took up the challenge and took turns rototilling the garden space.

Another time they chalked "Fuck Sally" on the outside wall of my classroom. I was in the garden with Eric, a precocious six year old right near the graffiti. He piped up: "Welcome to the Fuck Sally Show!" That was hilarious and robbed the taunt of its meanness. We laughed and laughed.

Years later, thirty years in fact, we had a reunion and we were all in a room together exchanging memories. One of the boys who had been so antagonistic stood up before all of us and apologized for his behavior at Pinel when he was young. "I'm now forty years old and I have

Laurel, Heather, Linsey, Sharon — Pinel Mudsliding 1971

my own children; that behavior was reprehensible and I am very sorry for it." His frank retraction prompted others to do the same. We teachers were amazed and thrilled.

The animals at Pinel are legendary. Pissbeard the goat was with us for years, smelly and ornery. Shorty the pony was a mainstay; Shelley, a nine-year-old-girl was his caretaker. She adored him and would ride him as fast as he would go, her hair flying in the wind. She would also snip his mane on the sly, and I had to disabuse her of that. One year Shelley married Shorty in the mock weddings we conducted on Valentine's Day. We held these weddings in the Big Room, and Shelley escorted her mate into the room for the ceremony.

Occasionally an animal would die of natural causes on the land. I assumed the job of gravedigger and buried the deceased with a small ritual. There were always lots of children with me at these solemnities.

The area around the school was not built up with houses at that time, and there were feral dogs that roamed the hills at night. Twice in the eight years I was at Pinel, these dogs massacred many of our animals: chickens, ducks even goats. When we arrived at school in the morning, I herded my young ones up the hill to our classroom distracting them with jokes and stories, so they didn't view the carnage.

My charges, the young children, were very cheerful and affectionate. We loved each other and had a good time learning lessons and playing together. The sandbox was humming with play and songs I would sing on my autoharp. I had a repertoire of folk songs of different ethnicities and countries. It was so enlightening and funny when years later one of the girls, Heather, wrote me a letter about singing "Zoom, golly, golly." Zum gali, gali is a Jewish song in Hebrew.

Our intent at the school was to stimulate the desire for learning and the self-discipline to pursue it. We felt if children were comfortable and happy and provided with sparks from adults who were kind and engaged with them, the kids would respond by participating in creative and educational activities. This approach worked! Some children were emotionally damaged from their previous school experience. We recognized this and allowed these children to play outside before we invited them to lessons in a classroom. Some wandered into classrooms on their own and saw their friends at work and joined in. Many of the graduates of Pinel pursued highly academic careers in their later years. We have an astrophysicist, a lawyer, who has a high-ranking position at Boalt Hall Law School, and many schoolteachers. Those who had less professional jobs chose to work at things they enjoyed. This was our goal: to educate children to pursue their dreams and live happy lives.

1968 Melts Into 1969

As 1968 drew to a close I felt reborn, rejuvenated, reinvented as a Pinel schoolteacher, a Berkeleyite, a woman pursuing her dreams. My journals are filled with accounts of nighttime dreams, I Ching readings, and my study of astrology. I was searching within and without to find my true self. I loved uncovering the layers of consciousness. I had not finished with LSD; there were a few more trips to come. I smoked pot and danced to my heart's content at parties and street fairs. I remember the teenaged Sheila Escovedo—now Sheila E, a well-known drummer—smiling widely as she played her congas with a street band; she was enjoying herself mucho. Other women musicians inspired me, especially pianists with their electric pianos rocking out in the clubs and in the streets with their bands. Some groups were all women. A particularly offbeat and intriguing group was named "Eyes." They dressed wildly with feathers and spangles and used dark makeup to look mysterious. Music was calling me; I had no plans to get a piano, but then…

In February 1969 it was raining. To my surprise an old upright piano appeared on the porch of the house around the corner from me. I knocked on the door to see why this instrument was outside in the inclement weather. A tall, middle-eastern man answered and said I could have the piano for $60, and he would help with moving it to my place. He and five of my men friends pushed, pulled, lifted, and dragged this behemoth to my second floor apartment. I vowed to always use piano movers when I saw what was involved. The piano, which weighed at least 500 pounds, had to be tipped on end to get around the narrow staircase turn. Fortunately all went well and the movers and the piano survived without a scratch.

Good fortune was in my stars. While I pursued my career as a teacher, this piano offered me the chance to get started on my next career as a musician. I was not making plans or setting goals as some do, I did what came naturally to me. I was going with the flow of my life. I was following my bliss. I loved being a teacher of young children, and if it were possible to have something more, it would be as a piano teacher and musician.

I had been so torn in my marriage, so ambivalent, so unclear as to what to do. I left Ron several times, then came back. But once I made the final decision to break away for good and forge my own life it was a steady stream of successes. I liked being on my own. I felt confident that I could invent my life. I could be independent.

The job I had at Pinel was very fulfilling. My charges, the five to nine year olds, were so loving and receptive. My colleagues were totally supportive. The school was written up in the San Francisco Chronicle. It was an important experiment and we all felt we were doing something significant. It was very innovative to let the children play outside most of the day. The lessons of reading, writing and arithmetic were short and tailored to the ability and the interests of the child. I used several methods to teach reading. The primers I used had simple stories about what children like to do. The first one was called Swings. The illustrations were photographs of children on swings. Then came Slides and Bikes.

I also followed Sylvia Ashton Warner's "organic reading" method. Each day I asked each child what word

Sallie's classroom at Pinel — 1969

they would like to know and wrote the word on a card. Over the weeks they built up a vocabulary of thirty or so words, and then I wrote stories with each one's vocabulary. Another method used rhyming words and a Program Reader. The children worked in these books themselves, using a wide bookmark that covered the answers to the questions. They checked themselves by exposing the answers. I read a lot of stories to the kids every day, even The Hobbit, which all children enjoyed; the older children (ten to thirteen) came to my classroom for that. Twice a year, I collected original stories from children of all ages and put out a storybook using the ditto machine. Notes from the Muddy Ground, Silver Bells and Cockle Shells, Red Wagon, I still have tattered copies of these gems. The older children made their own publications, usually hilarious, always creative. One group of girls put out The Horney Horse, with droll illustrations and zany stories of horses and their social life.

The older children also wrote and performed plays for the whole school drawing deeply on the current social movements. One holiday play featured Mrs. Santa Claus, who did the bidding of her husband and the elves that opposed him through their union. These precocious kids were spot-on in identifying hypocrisy and sexism in the late '60s and early '70s.

Sometimes busloads of people interested in a school like ours would arrive in the driveway to observe, take notes, and question the teachers about the goings on. We didn't allow toy guns at Pinel but some boys would carry sticks and pieces of wood as simulations. Bill liked to tell the story of his answer to questions about the parades of these warriors. "Those are the children of the peace activists who allow no war games at home," he explained.

I often meandered down the road to Briones Park with my charges. We found peace and quiet, nature, and cows in that lovely place. We would examine trees and plants, watch birds, walk through the herd of cows, climb trees and eat lunch as I told stories.

* * *

In Berkeley in 1969 a communal food-buying club was formed: The Food Conspiracy. It was citywide and broken down into neighborhood groups. Organic farmers were sought out and people delegated to purchase fruits and vegetables from them. In the neighborhood we filled out lists of what we wanted each week and then submitted the total to the larger group: The All Conspiracy. The food was delivered to a point house in each neighborhood where, on a certain days, we came to pick up our orders. It was a magnificent, socialistic system; all voluntary, no one was paid. Money was only used to buy the food; everyone was on the honor

Zack, Sallie, Willard — Pinel 1970

system. The Food Conspiracy lasted three to five years and then several local health food stores were founded, "Ma Revolution" was one. Local restaurants sprang up like "Omnivore."

We learned so much in this venture. At first we took turns leading a meeting and asking: "Who will pick up the produce?" "Who will pick up the cheese?" "Who will compile the list of produce each week?" People didn't volunteer right away and the leader became frustrated. So we tried another method that worked beautifully: we had a potluck lunch or dinner and passed around a sheet of paper with the jobs needed. Voila! The list was all filled in by the time we finished eating.

I was becoming very close friends with Maud, a neighbor across the street. She had a young daughter and when she heard from me about Pinel she sent her daughter to our school. Maud was an artist and an astrologer and tarot card reader. We had that common interest in the spiritual side of life, and we loved to dance and cavort. Maud was a great cook and knew how to make healthy foods taste delicious. She would steam kale, dress it with oil and vinegar and throw in walnuts: easy, nutritious and yummy. She painted taxis for the hippie taxi company: Taxis Unlimited. Her taxis were colorfully decorated with solar system planets and occult symbols. She once painted a harpsichord with flowers and designs—it was exquisite.

One night a new acquaintance came to my place for some Food Conspiracy business. Pamela was a dark-haired beauty with penetrating eyes and mind. She dressed with pizazz and good taste. Maybe a deep red satin top with a purple scarf, wide, silky, black pants and silver jewelry. She loved my apartment with its crazy colors and my two cats. As we talked I felt a strong urge to introduce her to Maud across the street. Maud was amenable and available. As we came into Maud's room the moon was rising in the sky out the window and a wonderful tarot reading was waiting for us on the carpeted floor. We bonded. We had years of fun together, talking and laughing, dancing and hiking. We communed. We are still in touch.

I heard of a woman who had kittens for adoption in my neighborhood. There were four or five adorable ones. This kitten would be a companion for Krishna

Food Conspiracy Pickup — 1970

Murphy. I decided on the runt of the litter. He was the smallest and the scruffiest of the bunch. A devilish kitten, he kept me and Krishna Murphy on our toes, so I named him Lucifer.

People's Park, 1969

In 1969, Telegraph Avenue was a bustling, hustling place. Street vendors sold their tie-dyed shirts, handmade jewelry, nature photographs, Rastafarian hats and tee shirts. There was a terrific secondhand thrift store where I bought a pea coat for $10 that lasted years. There was an excitement in the air; we were breaking with convention. People dressed in colorful, nonconformist outfits. Super-feminine, lacey dresses with lots of jewelry or cut-off jeans and old tee shirts. It felt like freedom on the streets in Berkeley. We could dress and act as we pleased. We were not tied to fashion or restricted by religious or social mores. A few people were naked.

People scurried in and out of Moe and Shakespeare's bookshops, buying and selling books, noting lectures and classes coming up. Telephone poles were covered with posters announcing rock band dances and political rallies. The street teemed with people, stoned and straight, hippies, college students, tourists, neighborhood folks. I'm sure many were selling their cannabis products too—I had my own connection on my block.

The University of California at Berkeley had appropriated some land just east of Telegraph Avenue, but the proposed construction of a dormitory had faltered and the land became derelict. It was an eyesore, weedy, muddy, garbage strewn, a dumping ground for old cars. After a year, in the spring of 1969, some activists declared that land could be a "People's Park," user developed and for use by all. Everyone thought that was a great idea and work began. We gathered day and night to break up the rubble, clean out the garbage and old cars, to plant trees, flowers, and shrubs. No one was in charge; it was a loose, anarchistic project. We labored cooperatively with the goal of making a beautiful park.

"Do you think zinnias would look good here by this tree?" I asked a fellow gardener.

"Put them away from the tree," he replied, "zinnias love sun."

"What about a swing set for the kids?" suggested a healthy, strong looking guy.

"Good idea. I'll bring my crew tomorrow and build it," said another.

The children worked as hard as we did digging, planting, and watering. People contributed hoses, shovels, rakes and other garden tools. Some brought seeds, others seedlings. "Wow, this is cool," a teenager commented "I'm working my butt off for fun." There was a strong camaraderie among us. We needed no overseer to plan and execute ideas. The physical labor of love inspired us. We shared the toil, the enthusiasm and the food and drinks and smokes we had after hours of work. It was very exciting to see something of beauty emerging from a garbage dump. After several weeks the land was transformed. Nature was blooming and people brought guitars to play and sing and celebrate.

Then, the University wanted the land back to build a sports-facility. The Chancellor assured us he would not take action without notice to the public. But Ronald Reagan was the governor of California, and he was not pleased with the people taking over the land or the University's mild reaction. He ordered the California Highway Patrol and the Berkeley Police to fence in the park in the middle of the night.

The next day many people came to the fence to protest. A rally on campus planned for something else turned into a demand to "take back the park." The community, the students, the activists, and neighbors involved were pitted against a phalanx of armed police. Not a pretty picture. Inevitably the protesters demanding the fence be taken down clashed with the police, who lobbed tear gas at us and shots were fired. Later we learned a bystander on a rooftop was killed. I was not scared. There was strength in numbers, but teargas burns the eyes and skin, and I found myself running away from the gas in the company of Tom Hayden, a well-known activist. We dispersed but the dispute was not over.

Everyday people went to the fence to push back and express dissatisfaction for the retraction of our park. People talked with each other, strategized, shouted slogans, and carried signs. Some attempted to engage the policemen, many of whom were young like we were.

"Why are you opposing us? You are one of us."

"We want to play in a park, what's wrong with that?"

Women put flowers on the bayonets and teased the young cops. "Don't you want to join us for dancing on the grass?"

"Do you always do what your daddy says?"

The cops were stone-faced and stood stiffly at these attempts at conversation.

For weeks we were an occupied city. Reagan ordered the National Guard into Berkeley. They drove around in open trucks, soldiers with rifles standing in the back surveying us. To what purpose? Were we so dangerous? Young people, older people, children wanting to play in a park? I felt that intimidation to be so unfair. It saddened me to see soldiers patrolling our city. To us People's Park was a service to the community; this extreme reaction was unwarranted.

Several weeks later we had permission from the City of Berkeley for a march from People's Park to Provo Park in downtown Berkeley. Thirty thousand people came, locals and people from all over California and other states. All came together to show support for our People's Park. My friend Tigger and I went with her two children, who attended Pinel School. We held hands in the crowd and were overwhelmed by the love and peacefulness of the marchers. We knew we were not alone in wanting a small, simple place to be a user developed park rather than another tentacle of the university dominating the neighborhood.

Years later, the City of Berkeley leased the land from the University and the fence was taken down. Another tract of land was leased from BART, which had been known as People's Park Annex, and turned into public space. There we have a sport's field, open space, a children's park and a dog park. Our work had not been in vain.

In August of 1969, the Woodstock Music Festival in Bethel, New York exemplified the peace and love ethos of our hippie generation. For three days and nights four hundred thousand people listened to thirty-two bands, danced, cavorted around and with good humor put up with a rainstorm that turned the grassy field into a muddy basin. When the food supply dwindled the families in the nearby town helicoptered in fresh supplies. It was an amazing display of goodwill by so many people.

The Rolling Stones were on a concert tour of the country in 1969 and decided to end their tour with a free concert in the Bay Area. It was a last minute idea and decisions were made hastily; no one thought the whole thing through with any deliberation. The venue was confirmed two days before the event on December 9th. It would be at the Altamount Speedway in Livermore, east of Berkeley.

Tigger and I were ready to go at a moment's notice. How exciting to have another musical and countercultural event happen in our area. We took her two children, Holly and John, ages 6 and 8. The day was overcast with clouds—dreary. As we approached the entrance we saw that people were parking and walking. We did the same. As we trudged along; I felt like it was a hippie refugee camp. It was gloomy and people were not enthused and joyous. The fields were dry and brown. There were no food concessions or colorful tents and banners as in other gatherings. The Hell's Angels milled around the stage and that was disturbing. Later they tried to control people, poking them with pool cues. Hundreds of people were already sitting on the lackluster grass, so we climbed the hill and found a place to park ourselves. Happily we brought food and drink to enjoy.

Finally some music began around noon. We were so far away we could hardly see the stage. When the Jefferson Airplane was playing someone said into the microphone:

"There's a fight here on the stage, please help us stop it before someone gets hurt." We were surprised, but the mass of people in front of us blocked our view; we couldn't see what was going on. I walked around our area and realized there were a lot of bad drugs here. No one was aggressive to me, but the happy, exuberant mood of events in Golden Gate Park and Telegraph Avenue was absent here.

The Rolling Stones waited until darkness fell to appear on the stage. To me, this was Mick Jagger's ego trip. He wanted to portray himself as Lucifer, the god of darkness. The audience was restless and tired of waiting for the Stones. Fires had been started in garbage cans around the periphery of the field. There was an ominous feeling, and we held the children's hands as we moved towards the stage. There were three hundred thousand people, we learned later, and the masses were not in a gay mood. A sleeping dragon was more like it. Down by the stage people were disgruntled and we learned the next day, someone had been killed. Mick called for us to "cool out," and finally he commanded, "Sit down!" We sat and then he sang "Under My Thumb." That did it for me and the Rolling Stones. What an arrogant message. I never bought another album.

Eventually we walked slowly in the teeming crowd back to the car. We were happy to be together but not elated by the day's experience.

Life and Death in 1971

At Pinel we had two four-day camping trips for the whole school: at the beginning of the school year and at the end. During the year, Bill, Jim, and Ray took a group of older children on a three-week camping trip. Bill went to Vancouver Island in Canada, Jim and Ray went to Havasupai Canyon in Arizona.

After I had been at Pinel three years, I asked Bill if I could go on his Canada trip. He agreed and my charges were assigned to other teachers and student teachers for those three weeks. We drove up to Canada in three or four cars, bringing food and supplies including large cooking pots and pans. Carol, a student teacher from Antioch College, and several parents came along too.

It was April and it was raining on Vancouver Island. The teachers had sturdy tents as did some of the kids and others doubled and tripled up in tube tents. The unlucky ones on the ends of those tents got wet. None of the children got sick, but Carol was feeling unwell, so I accompanied her to the National Health Clinic in Victoria; our campground was not far from that city. It was Easter Sunday, but the clinic was open and treated foreigners for free. I noticed a poster for an "Easter Be-in at Beacon Hill Park." After her appointment Carol felt better so we walked to the park. The weather had cleared and the sun shone brightly on the lush grass and made the surrounding waters sparkle. As we approached the group of people sitting on the grass and singing, I noticed a young man in a tie-dyed thermal shirt and a long blond braid down his back playing guitar. I joined the dancers right away and caught the eye of that guitar player. I danced with a young girl with dark hair and shining eyes. She was a precocious eleven year old, Ann-Marie Moore, and we enjoyed talking to each other. I also engaged the guitar player in conversation and found out he was a draft-dodger from California. We had an immediate attraction to each other. After awhile I told Carol I would be late coming back to the campground, and Bruce and I left the park hand in hand. When we arrived at the home where he was staying, there was Ann Marie! Her mother Judith, a woman of my age, opened her home to draft-dodgers and Bruce lived there. We had a great time talking, eating, feeling comfortable with each other.

Bruce and I found other places to commune and make love over the next two weeks. I had brought my diaphragm along just in case, naughty girl that I was. Bruce also came to our campground and hiked with the kids and other teachers. He fit right in with my extended family as I did with his. We were on the same wavelength.

Several weeks after I returned to Berkeley, I found myself pregnant. This was unexpected—not what I had in mind. I agonized over my plight, because even though it was not what I wanted, I was thirty-two, and I knew this was my last chance to have a baby.

In my journal, I spilled out my distress, my suffering. I listed the possibilities: baby, abortion. I had an I Ching reading: The Darkening of the Light. That fit my mood. I wrote this in my journal:

I burn a candle for my love   for my baby   still unborn

I love you for my life you are a friend of

mine

I cry too much now   it's so sad

tears flow like blood   bloodlines

Placentas   propinquity

it needs more time   a better space

Oh love baby I want

you   in my mind I still need a place to go

Helpless   helpless

I called Bruce and told him. I suggested I come up to the island for a quick weekend to discuss this turn of events. He liked that idea. We had a very sweet camping time on the beach. We fantasized about the baby: how smart she/he would be, how musical, how creative, how beautiful! But in the end, Bruce admitted he was too young. "I'm 22 and not ready to become a father. I haven't figured out what to do with my life. It's just not the right time for me." I accepted that and having no desire to raise a child alone, I made an appointment for an abortion at Kaiser. Just a few months earlier the procedure was legalized. The date was mid-June.

In early June, the Pinel school bus pulled into the school parking lot after the end of the year camping trip. Someone rushed over to the bus and said to me, "Sallie your brother Fred is on the phone." Bad news.

"Sit down Sallie," said Fred, "your daddy's dead. Daddy died last night. There's a ticket for you to come home tonight at the San Francisco Airport," Fred announced in his no-nonsense manner. I was devastated. Daddy was sixty-seven, he had retired from AT&T two years before, and we all had high hopes that he would enjoy not working and get more involved in his house projects or his garden or cultivate other interests. But no, he had never solved his depression problem and had ended up drinking more often than when he was working.

I threw a few things in a bag, asked Maud to feed and pet Krishna and Lucifer and off I went. On the flight I had a dream:

I am walking around the frame of a house being built: Bill, Jim, and Ray are there. They are urging me on, cautioning me to be careful, to walk on the strong planks. I am slow, there are many holes, deep crevices, loose boards, but they tell me I do know the way. I realized in the dream that Daddy was gone, and now I had Bill, Jim, and Ray to guide me. They were not substitutes for Daddy, they were mentors.

At the funeral home there was an open casket. I wrote in my journal:

my daddy has a rose in his hands
a rose he nurtured   a rose he tended   a rose for my daddy
his spirit hovers heavy around his body I am filled up with his spirit
I am brimming over with tears with love   with sobs

Mother was very distraught and cried all the time. "He was the nicest man I ever met," she moaned through her tears. I had the I Ching book with me to do a reading for Mother. She received "Before Completion: The conditions are difficult, the task is great and full of responsibility. It is nothing less than that of leading the world out of confusion. But it is a task that promises success." I think that reading comforted Mother—I certainly was.

The death of my dad took preference in my mind over the fact that I was pregnant. I needed to return to Berkeley soon for the termination. I stayed as long as possible and made an excuse to Mother that I needed to see my doctor about a "female problem." My mother was so grief-stricken she didn't ask more about that. My brothers were there to console her. I was reluctant to leave, but the urgency of my situation compelled me.

And so the deed was done.

Now indeed I am emptied of fullness and full of emptiness

this the great void   the universe "the more we take of it, the more remains"

I am drained   now physically weakened walk so slowly

don't faint   be careful and always think- no blood I bleed easily

kept me in the recovery room   I fainted on the floor   blood in the toilet

I was suffering, but I knew I had done the right thing for me. As much as I longed for a child of my own, I wanted a partner, a father for the child to go on that journey with me. I believed the circle of the family needed two parents.

Later that summer, amnesty was declared for draft-dodgers of the Vietnam War. Bruce came home.

What a joy to see him, talk to him, commiserate with him, and be held in his arms. I invited him to live with me in my apartment. He liked that idea. Mother did not. When I told her I was living with my boyfriend, she replied huffily, "I don't approve of couples living together unmarried."

Maybe that was the reason I was not invited to go to Mississippi with her and my brothers to inter Daddy's ashes at the Rhyne Family Cemetery in Lexington, Mississippi. I'll never know. But I was not bothered or offended by that, for I had had a message from Daddy in a dream:

I was living as an adult at 624-11th Street in Brooklyn where I grew up. My father was dead on the floor in his and mother's bedroom. Time went by in the dream, a week. I understood then that it was my duty to take care of the body. So I entered the bedroom and knelt down by the corpse. Now, it looked like a fetus and not very pleasant. Undeterred and not repulsed, I knew it was Daddy; I reached out to pick it up. As soon as I touched it, the creature turned into the face of my Dad as a young man. He had dark hair and a dark moustache, my handsome father. He was beaming at me. The non-verbal message was that this was the way he wanted me to remember him.

This dream was so vivid and meaningful to me. I was fulfilled by this communication from my dad. I needed no burial ceremony for closure. It was clear to me that Daddy's spirit was alive beyond the grave and he thought of me.

Diversity at Pinel

In 1969, the Rosenberg Foundation granted funds to Pinel School to bring black, brown, and foster children to Pinel every day for two summers and once a week during the school year. The founders of Pinel applied for the grant in order in enhance the lives of the one hundred, white suburban kids who attended our school. There had been one black boy from Berkeley in the beginning, and the teachers now realized the need for an infusion of diversity from a new group of sixty-two children of color.

The black kids were bussed from Pittsburg, California, city children who dubbed Pinel "the school in the weeds." The first day most of those children did not leave the bus that brought them. They saw nothing attractive, nothing they wanted to do outside their bus. Slowly over that first week, some white kids got on the bus and told the black kids what was going on at the school. There was fort-building, art projects including ceramics, general hanging out, ball games, climbing the tower on the hill, and getting together as a group in the library to share experiences. Gradually the black kids came along and joined activities. When the Mexican-American children cooked lunch everyone was happy. Tacos and enchiladas were great levelers. The Latino kids were from Oakland.

Demetrius was a tall, athletic black boy, eleven or twelve years old, who organized ball games and was very sociable to all. Tanya was a younger, feistier black girl, who pooh-poohed activities until she got involved and then participated eagerly. There were happy days and tension times between the children. There are pictures of

Stirling, a blonde white boy, wrestling with José, a brown kid from Oakland, both around nine or ten years old. It was a steamy, physical battle with no serious consequences and grins at the end. They both enjoyed it! And a wonderful series of pictures of Tanya and the white girl, Laurel, on two swings with their legs entwined, being pushed by Marta, a brown girl from Oakland. They are all smiling broadly.

The all-school camping trip we took that fall was to Sequoia National Park in central California. We had to truck in water as there was no running water at our campsite. At first, the city children from Pittsburg and Oakland were horrified. Sleeping on the ground, using the outhouse, insects flying around, this was not their cup of tea. After a few days, however, they were cavorting around with the more experienced campers. They hiked and swam in the stream, they sang along lustily at the campfire and relished the scary ghost stories Jim and Ray told after the music. We teachers were encouraged by the relationships that formed between some children. Some of these friendships continued after the program finished, and the black and brown kids were no longer at the school.

We hired a photographer to document this exciting endeavor. He assembled a beautiful and provocative book called *Yesterday I Learned There Was Forever*. The cover shows a blond girl helping a black boy set up his crochet needle. There was a photo of an older Pinel girl giving a Tarot reading to several black and brown kids. There are smiles and frowns, snakes and sand castles, eating and messy art projects, involvement by all.

* * * * * *

Batik project at Pinel — 1969

Laurel, Tanya, Maria — Pinel 1969

Bruce and I lived together for a year and then went our separate ways.

Shortly thereafter, I went to visit Judith and Ann Marie and family in Victoria, British Columbia, the family I met years before on a Pinel camping trip. We got along famously. I loved this family. I asked Judith if Ann Marie could come to Berkeley, live with me, and go to Pinel School. At eleven years of age, Ann Marie was precocious and her mother sensed she was pulling on her tether to the family, straining to get more freedom. Judith trusted and loved me and said yes to my request. Ann Marie was thrilled.

We were compatible housemates. My apartment was small but my pre-pubescent stepdaughter found spots for her treasures. Her dolls and little box homes were quartered under the table that served as my desk in the living/bed/music room. Paints and sketchpads showed up in the kitchen. At first, Ann Marie followed my schedule for being at home, washing the dishes, sweeping the floor. After a few months she rebelled and we had to work out an easier routine for her.

My best friend, Maud, lived across the street and had a daughter a few months younger than Ann Marie, who also went to Pinel School. The two girls became best friends and to this day are very close. Sharon and Ann Marie loved acting in plays. They pursued theater at Pinel and in the Emeryville Shakespeare Company based in Berkeley. They were fairies in a production of Midsummer's Night Dream totally indulging their talent for exaggerated movement and expression.

The next summer I returned Ann Marie to her family in Victoria. We all went on a lovely trip to the Okanogan

Valley on the mainland of British Columbia. Our campground was near a beautiful mountain lake surrounded by lush vegetation and tall trees. It was the year Germaine Greer's book *The Female Eunuch* was published, 1972, and I brought my copy along. I realized that Berkeley was a place where ideas of women's liberation and new social codes were discussed and practiced. Slowly the ideas migrated to other places and slowly the larger society was affected. My Canadian friends were new to these notions of women taking a greater role in society; they were interested but not passionately as I was.

A romance bloomed that summer between Tom and me. He was another American draft-dodger of the Vietnam War, who decided to stay in Canada. Tom was tall and lanky, with blond curls, and an infectious smile. He worked in a nursery and would one day have his own business growing and selling trees. Tom was very gentle and sweet. He and I melted into one another for a long distance romance that lasted a year. I visited him that winter, and we cossetted ourselves in a small log cabin in the woods. The trees were heavy with snow and groaned under the weight until the afternoon sun touched the branches and melted the white clumps, releasing the limbs upward with a sighing sound.

Tom wrote me beautiful letters often decorated with his drawings and watercolors. He had a young daughter from his marriage and the next summer the three of us went on a beautiful camping trip on the West Coast Trail near Victoria on Vancouver Island. The beach had no other human campers that we could see, and we ran around and swam naked in the warm sunshine. We built a little lean-to from driftwood to sleep in and generally frolicked in the surrounding natural world. One day we found a salmon washed up on the beach. Tom knew it was fresh from the fishing boats we saw out on the ocean. The scales of the fish were wholesome looking. We rejoiced in this gift from the ocean gods! Tom dug a sand pit and wrapped the salmon in aluminum foil we had in our cache. While the fish roasted under a small fire, we walked on the beach and greeted a young American guy who was passing through. He told us that President Nixon had resigned. We whooped it up together and invited this bearer of good news to our salmon feast. It became a celebration!

Back in Berkeley, I met a guitar player who lived across the street from me. Jack had a funky set up with his acoustic guitar and a small amp cobbled together with old rope and duct tape. He taught me what a seventh chord was and then we proceeded to the blues progression: all seventh chords. I had fun playing with Jack and we started to collect other musicians. A woman named Sallie, same spelling as I use, was one. She wrote humorous songs about men and women and relationships. We started the duo, Sallie and Sallie, and played at the Starry Plough Irish Pub two blocks down from my house. Sallie lived around the corner.

I had played Ragtime Piano at the Plough by myself on their old upright piano. People enjoyed it and so did I, but this was a new level—playing with other people. At one point there was a collection of characters, including me, called "Yuk City." We blasted away at our folk-rock songs and the patrons of the Irish Pub loved it! I had an arrangement of "St. Louis Blues" that was smashing!

My life was so full now: my work at Pinel, music, and love affairs. It was a far cry from the trying and turbulent times of my marriage. I wished Ron well but found myself cutting off ties with friends that still had some contact with him. I was reborn now and had to disconnect from that past life.

Ann-Marie Moore — Vancouver Island, 1971

Ann-Marie and Sallie — 1971

The 70s Roll Along

In the early 70s, we felt safe in my neighborhood. My door did not have a dead bolt. The outside door to the house was not locked. We didn't have crime like the larger cities of Oakland and San Francisco. Ours was a college town—intellectual, political, spiritual—not criminal. Then a woman on our street was mugged; her purse was ripped off, and she was knocked down by the thief. This happened in broad daylight. Alert! Several friends and I responded. We talked to Joan, the victim, and decided it was time to organize our neighborhood. We had the Food Conspiracy for sustenance, we needed a neighborhood watch group for safety. We made a flyer calling a meeting for the following week at a neighbor's home and went around putting this news under doors and in mailboxes.

Thirty-five people showed up for the meeting! This was impressive. Our neighbors were willing to be active. We wanted to prevent crime by being strong, aware, and vigilant. People had ideas. We would invite the police to our next meeting. We organized a phone tree. People would look out for each other and respond to cries for help.

When the police came to our next meeting we were surprised. They said, "Just call us, we'll take care of the situation." We did not believe that. We continued to organize and get to know each other. We liked each other. One neighbor put out a newsletter. We had a block party with volleyball, music, and food. A friend's mother from New York was going to stay in my apartment to care for my cats when I went away for the weekend, but she refused unless I installed a dead bolt on my door. I did.

Later someone broke into my upstairs neighbor's apartment. Hannah was away and I was watering her plants. I heard noises in her place and knew someone was in there. I opened my back door at the same time this intruder opened Hannah's back door, and there she was. I demanded, "Who are you?" She retreated. Hannah had nothing a thief wanted, no TV, no camera, only an old manual typewriter. When I called Hannah and described the woman she said, "No, I don't know anyone of that description." I knew then we had to lock the downstairs door to the house. Mr. Palmer, our landlord who lived downstairs was not willing to go to the expense of house wiring doorbells, but our rent was low, and I decided to do it myself. I rigged up a battery-operated system with large batteries on the upper ledges of our doors and wires along the wall down to the doorbells. It worked okay with occasional repairs in the rainy season.

Deakin Street where I lived in Berkeley was a short street: one block in Oakland, two blocks in Berkeley south of Ashby, one block north of Ashby. There was a block party on the north-end one weekend, with live dance music. Just what I liked to do: dance in the street. I found myself moving to the music with a lovely young man I hadn't seen before. We boogied with energy and felt a connection and an attraction, so Jim came into my life. He was a political activist, and soon we were doing things together—going door to door in an election, having dinner together and inevitably, ineluctably, making love. He was irresistible. And he was involved with other women. Fine, I had another boyfriend too, Bill, the photographer, who documented the diversification of Pinel for the two years we had the grant. Jim and I went camping together and attended a spiritual gathering at Winterland in San Francisco. That event filled me with such energy and physical excitement, I nearly exploded with love for my friend Jim and the whole universe.

My journals of the day are full of my desire for romance, for love making as well as a desire to keep my independence. I truly loved Bruce, Tom, and now Jim, but I kept advising myself to keep a certain distance in the relationships so as not to become dependent on my lovers. I shivered with delight when my love touched me and we fell into a passionate embrace. I usually wanted more of their time than I got, especially from Tom who lived in Canada. It was a conundrum: I didn't want to be married. Living with Bruce became restrictive sometimes, because I wanted more time alone, but I felt I needed the embrace more often than it occurred. I found fulfillment in sex by surrendering, and I urged myself not to give up my individuality in the relationship. I had surrendered all in the marriage with Ron and wanted never to do that again.

I have lost touch with all these lovely lovers except Jim. We are still friends and I love his wife as well. We have good times together around music and art.

In the 1970s women's consciousness raising groups were happening and one was organized in our neighborhood. It turned out that most of those women were married and were traditional in their approach: they wanted more freedom in their marriages, but they didn't relate to single women having love affairs or homosexual relationships. I organized a smaller group of women to meet at my house, and of course I included single women like me who had relationships with men outside of marriage.

I didn't yet know any open lesbians. We had an artist in our group and she suggested we each create a piece of art to express our rising female consciousness. I made a papier-mâché doll. One side was a sad-faced girl in a white dress with tears on her face and blood on her skirt. The other side was a happy hippie girl with a broad smile and a colorful shirt, her jeans had sunrays around her loins. I felt fortunate to live in a world where I had a satisfying job with children, the approval of my friends, and the love of my boyfriends. Nothing was perfect but love abounded.

I wanted to take my last LSD trip now. I had read about how you could program your experience just by telling yourself what you wanted to do and following that plan when you got high. I wanted to go back to my early childhood and see how my parents coped with me. I thought of it as a happy, even ecstatic early childhood, and I wanted to revisit it.

Maud and Peter lived across the street. We were all close friends, and they agreed to comfort and help me if I needed it. LSD was readily available from friends and even acquaintances. Once, I took Clear Light Acid on a strip of paper that I got from a young man who picked me up hitchhiking. It was a great trip, a pure blissful time. I don't recall where I got the acid for this last trip. I arranged the date and went across the street to explore my unconscious. Maud was painting a taxi for Taxi Unlimited on the street, Peter was doing things in their house, and they left me alone for my experiment. I felt myself a baby in a crib with high sides. I couldn't see Mother and Daddy, but I could hear them. They were talking about me in a delighted way. They were pleased with me and my growth and personality. Wow, I was joyful. It felt so good to be alive. At one point, I got a little nervous and ran across the street to my apartment without disturbing my two friends. After I had checked up on my kitties, I came back to Maud and Peter's place and wandered into Sharon's room. Sharon was Maud's daughter. She was twelve or thirteen and her bedroom was neat and cozy with colorful curtains and bedspread and stuffed animals set up on her bed. I snuggled up with these stuffed animals and had the realization that "all is well!" I felt satisfied with my life, grateful for my parents and content that I would keep on exploring my dreams and creating my life as I went along on my path.

Maud painting a taxi — 1970

Dancing in the Street

In Berkeley in the late 1960s and early 1970s, dancing in the street was happening most weekends. Local bands played for free and people exchanged energy with the musicians by dancing joyously in front of them. One lovely, sunny day, I was dancing to a local rock band on Telegraph Avenue with Lisa, a friend from the neighborhood. We were lost in the bliss of the music and the good vibes; pot smoke wafted around open, friendly people. After a while two young men came over to talk to us.

"We're making a film," they informed us. "We'd like you two to be in it."

The film was about the goddess of the sea, Andromeda. In one scene, two women make love to each other in a bower of flowers on a hillside. Lisa and I were flattered, but we explained that since we were heterosexual we wouldn't make a convincing lesbian couple. The guys took our phone numbers and called a few days later to say they had found a lesbian couple and wanted us to dance around them as they embraced. "Yes!" Lisa and I were thrilled.

A few weeks later, we all piled into a car and headed for the Marin hills. It was a beautiful day and the hills were a glorious green with soft grass and bushes, here and there the oak trees cast their shadows. We all got stoned with pot, ate something, and got to work! The lesbian couple were relaxed and tenderly made love as Lisa and I floated around them exulting in the glory of nature's gifts. There might have been a flute player piping sweet melodies to inspire us all.

A few months later, we went to a screening of the film

at a small art gallery. The opening scene shows a young man in a coarse, brown, woolen cloak striding through the woods with a walking stick. He makes his way to the sea seeking the goddess. There is music but no talking in the film. The man falls asleep on the beach and our scene is his dream. When he wakes he realizes the goddess loves women. She has left him a conch shell. This charming remembrance was for him though his quest was for naught.

Months later we heard that Grove Press had bought this short, art film and a check for $25 was slipped under my door.

Lisa and I had known each other for a year or so. We took a Tai Chi class with the wonderful, eccentric Master Choy at the Shattuck Avenue Coöp. We were interested in Eastern thought and physical disciplines. We read and admired Carl Jung. We kept dream journals.

One day Lisa told me she had just met a well-known San Francisco Chronicle journalist, who also lived in our neighborhood. She invited me to dinner to meet him. I was surprised: he was not very friendly. He spoke arrogantly, and was unappealing physically, overweight, and looked older in an unattractive way. Lisa had indicated she was attracted to him when she talked about him. I recognized the name even though I only read the Berkeley Barb newspaper. This man never spoke directly to me but made an oblique remark indicating he knew I was there.

Lisa was excited to have met this man, because his circle of friends included Jungian analysts and college professors who studied and taught the ideas we were learning about. "All of a sudden," she said, "I am in a world of people who are professionally involved in the philosophies I've been reading about."

O brave new world, That has such people in't.

(Shakespeare: The Tempest)

One day I stopped in at her place to discover that she had moved and left no message as to her whereabouts. I never heard from her again. I hoped her rise in status was fulfilling, kept her dancing, and made her happy.

The Magical Pygmy Forest

The Pygmy Forest was the perfect place for an acid trip. I felt comfortable and safe with my friends in an unthreatening environment: no poisonous plants or animals. The trees were so reassuring. They were small and you could cuddle them. They were benign beings. I remember being high and down on my hands and knees examining the forest floor, then popping up to view the landscape and seeing a fellow traveler foraging around in the bushes across the path.

Pygmy Forest — 1967

There are many patches of pygmy forest in northern California. Patsy's patch was near the town of Mendocino. I often got a ride there from the Bay Area. The last leg of the long drive wound around stretches of the rolling golden hills and through the deep, shady forests of tall, lacey pines, and redwood trees. Finally the coastline would come into view, beautiful steep cliffs plunged down to the shore of the Pacific Ocean. Squawks of sea gulls filled the air, hawks soared through the fresh salty breezes. The telephone poles were all numbered and just before the town of Mendocino we would turn right, up a road, to pole 53. We parked and made our way into the pygmy on rocky, hardscrabble paths. Little by little over the years our friends cleared paths to their cottages in the forest. They used no backhoes or other machines; it was all cleared by hand, backbreaking work.

Patsy and Gordon's place was makeshift but a comfortable lodging, not built to code but a cozy, livable dwelling with a loft. Toilet facilities were outside: a platform on the ground with a covered hole. Patsy trucked in manure and compost for her stand of marijuana, a vegetable garden and colorful flowers around the front of her house. "The pygmy sucks up all the nutrients," she told us. Feeding was ongoing.

The pygmy has grey and dusty acidic soil; the trees and bushes are therefore stunted. The pines are six or seven feet high at the most. You can circle the trunk with your hand. The needles are green and healthy but short. The rhododendrons are miniature and have lovely, little blossoms in the spring. The huckleberries are tiny and delicious. When Patsy and Gordon, and Jack and Mardi bought several acres in 1969, the forest was not protected by the government; soon after, it was declared a National Monument.

Jack and Mardi's place was a short walk away from Patsy and Gordon's. The trees and shrubs of the pygmy were not high, but they were dense and provided privacy for the residents. If you kept walking west past Jack's place, you noticed the plants and trees were growing taller, greener, more lush. At one point you stepped over an imaginary line and into the Van Damme State Park: tall magnificent redwoods and verdant, lush ferns, walk through the park and you come to the beach: the Pacific Ocean.

On one LSD trip, I walked through the pygmy to the ocean by myself. I had been feeling a little shaky: "Am I alive? Am I in a dream? Am I a solid creature?" When I got to the beach I sat down in a rocky, sandy place. I held some rocks in my hands. I felt the outline of each rock and the weight of all of them. It seemed that the rocks spoke to me, their weight grounded me. "Yes," I thought, "I'm as solid as I can be. I'm not going to float away. These rock friends are anchoring me, their weight is my focus."

The pygmy forest was truly magical at night with a full moon. The white, dusty paths glowed in the moonlight. The trees rustled their hellos, the occasional birdsong was music. I felt at home, at peace, and in awe of nature's beauty.

Patsy was the focal point of my social experiences in the pygmy. She was English, stood six feet tall, and was lovely to look at. Patsy was as gracious and friendly as she was beautiful. She was a marvelous cook and would always have delicious meals and snacks for all her visitors.

Patsy provided a welcome and nurturing environment for all who happened by her home. She had a son from her first marriage to Fred, and now she recently birthed another with her new partner, Gordon.

Patsy took me to the wonderful pond a few miles from her home. It was a large, quiet country spot with hundreds of frogs. Bullfrogs bellowed their greetings and mating calls. Dragonflies zoomed around. The air was thick with natural smells and sounds. A woods surrounded this rustic eden and everyone swam naked. There was an anchored raft in the bushes at the edge of the pond, and couples swam out there to be private in their lovemaking.

I had a rich and rewarding time with Patsy, her family and friends, and with the exotic landscape of the pygmy forest.

More On The 70s—Ways of Meringue

I was thoroughly immersed in the counterculture in my neighborhood and in my life. My job was at an alternative school; I bought my food at the Food Conspiracy. We had succeeded in organizing our neighborhood. My drug of choice was grass, and I very occasionally took acid. Every so often I attended a counterculture event with the luminaries of our culture: Timothy Leary, Allen Ginsberg, and Ram Dass, as Richard Alpert was now called.

One evening I went to see Timothy Leary. It was in North Berkeley at a place with a large stage and seating for maybe two-hundred people. The place was full. Our hero was talking at the podium on stage about "Turning On, Tuning In and Dropping Out" when the audience became aware of a lovely, young woman walking slowly down the aisle towards the stage. She was naked. Leary kept talking as she approached. When she mounted the stage, he turned to her and asked, "What is your sign?" —meaning her astrological sign. I don't remember what she answered, but he managed to talk her into taking a seat on a couch behind him. A young man from the audience joined her and got naked. Leary's wife, Rosemary, came out from backstage and sat on the couch with them. The program went on. Leary finished his talk. Questions were asked and answered. The young woman looked taken aback that her daring deed had not caused a stir. We were cool.

Another event was called "Wake Up." It was at the student union building on the University of California Berkeley's campus. About fifty or so of us chanted "Om Mani Padme Hum" and grooved together. We sent goodwill and support to Timothy Leary who was then in trouble with the authorities. "Wake Up" was the call of Buddhists to become aware of our true existence outside the ordinary workaday world. We could find fulfillment and bliss if we meditated, chanted for world peace, and pursued the road to self-awareness and deep consciousness. These practices have a wonderful relaxing effect; I still practice today.

My musical development was proceeding apace. Lessons with a jazz pianist led me to the Bach Inventions: beautiful pieces that taught independence of hands to the pianist. I read through jazz arrangements of tunes like "Lush Life," an advanced jazz composition, to learn how the chords are played in the style. Herbie Hancock and Chick Correa were the young jazz lions I listened to. My unconscious spirit guides were at work too. For no apparent reason I decided to buy an electric piano. The Fender Rhodes was the hip sound, so I looked and found one at a reasonable price. My friend Ed drove me in his station wagon to the seller's house. It was perfect. We carried this 100-pound instrument down the stairs to his car and up the stairs to my place. Ouch! That was the start of back problems. At 110 pounds myself, I thought I was an Amazon woman. Not.

My landlord who lived downstairs and the two women who had apartments in the house could hear me practicing. Hannah, my upstairs neighbor was a college professor and an author. She never complained; I think she enjoyed it, and when she was working she tuned it out. Once she slipped a New Yorker cartoon under my door. It showed a young girl at a piano recital saying, "And now for my encore, Scott Joplin's Sunflower Slow Drag." But my downstairs neighbor was not so amused.

She complained to Mr. Palmer, our landlord about the "noise." Mr. Palmer wanted us to work it out ourselves. I said I would play under my headphones on the electric piano every other night and use the acoustic piano on the off nights. That worked.

I named my Fender Rhodes "Angie." After three abortions I had still thought I might have a child someday. Now I knew I would not. Angie was my baby. My creation would be music. The electric piano equipped me for a rock band, although I had never consciously thought about that. Lo and behold, friends told me that a women's rock band was looking for a pianist who had a keyboard. I auditioned for The Ways of Meringue and was accepted. This was amazing to me because my experience with playing electric music was zilch. All the music I had played at the Starry Plough was acoustic, no amplifiers.

The Ways of Meringue got their crazy name from a conversation between two of the members. One was trying to make a lemon meringue pie and having little success making the meringue peak up stiffly. "Ah," said the other, "You have to know the Ways of Meringue." Eventually a friend of the band made a beautiful embroidered banner that hung on my piano, of a lemon meringue pie with a woman flying out of the meringue.

Lorraine, the drummer, was a talented songwriter and the band played her original pieces. Debbie, the guitarist was a melodic, tasteful soloist who soared to the heights in her improvs like Jerry Garcia in the Grateful Dead. She also made chord charts of the popular rock and funk songs we wanted to play. Debbie at age nineteen, was the youngest member of the group. I was the oldest at thirty-six.

Maureen, the electric bassist, was my best buddy in the band. She kept me on track in the songs with her bass notes. These three women, the founders of the band were lesbians. Lydia the singer was married to a man who came to all rehearsals and all gigs. She left the band shortly after I came and Lynn, a friend of Maureen's joined us as the singer.

At this time there was a subculture of gay women and men, who were proud of their sexual identity. There were many gay and lesbian clubs where people danced, listened to music, hung out and flirted and matched up with others. I had not been aware of this subculture, and now I was plopped down into it. What fun!

Lorraine's partner was Marcia, a friend and promoter of the group. Maureen and Debbie were a pair. Lynn had a husband and I was the independent. I never invited my boyfriends to the gigs. Nervousness was a problem for me in the beginning. I calmed down after a few months, realizing it was a supportive group; we were not competing with each other. I could proceed and grow at my own rate. That was a relief.

My bandmates were fun to be with. They laughed and cut up at the rehearsals although we also got down to business and learned songs, made arrangements and thought about new songs. We rehearsed in Lorraine's basement. Once my mother was visiting and I brought her along. She sat outside in a chair. The music was so loud! We had a gig when Mother was here. We played at a Catholic girl's high school dance in San Francisco. I arranged a ride for Mother with Pat, a good friend. After two songs Mother asked Pat, "Isn't the music very loud?"

"Yes," she said. "Are you ready to leave?"

"Let's go!" answered Mother.

1975

In 1975 Pinel was changing. Enrollment was down for several reasons. The cost of living was rising, and although Pinel was very reasonable in its monthly fee, it was an extra expense for middle-class families. The interest in progressive schools like Pinel was waning among those families with income for private school. The pendulum was swinging back to more disciplined, even militaristic schools. Academic studies were now more desirable to those parents than the play-based curriculum of Pinel. We felt our approach did not inhibit academic interest in the children; when they were ready they became involved in more intellectual pursuits. Alice Kenney, Bill's wife whom I replaced as the little kids teacher in 1968 was back. Alice offered American History, Egyptian history, and advanced reading studies to the older students who signed up enthusiastically.

Bill Kenney had moved on to another job and Jim Stein had also left to pursue other projects. Alice, Ray, and I, plus our student teachers, were the teaching and administrative staff now. There was tension in this group. Jim had been Ray's best friend and Ray missed him. Bill had been our charismatic leader, bringing humor and harmony to our group. The joyous, ebullient feeling that had greeted me in 1968 had altered. I was aware of these changes and still very dedicated to Pinel, but I was also distracted by my involvement in The Ways of Meringue.

The band was a happening group! We had gigs galore at gay bars and other clubs all with large stages and dance floors. The Starry Plough had no stage at that time, the patrons and the musicians were on the floor together. Having a stage engendered stage fright in me. I didn't think I knew enough or had the requisite experience to be on a stage. There's a picture of the band at "Jerry's Stop Sign," a club on University Avenue in Berkeley. I look frightened and uptight. Happily, experience and study improved my mental state, and I look relaxed in later photos. We played Lorraine's original songs and cover tunes by the Doobie Brothers, Mott The Hoople, Earth, Wind and & Fire and others. These women were not man-haters; they loved rock'n roll music and appreciated the expertise of the men players. Indeed we tried to emulate those men players with our own twist.

We took publicity pictures—8 by 10 glossies—to make posters for our gigs. At first we dressed very casually. Lynn, the singer, wore her overalls, Debbie had on a man's shirt and jeans. Later we were gussied up in spangly outfits we borrowed, and we felt more professional. We had gigs in town and out of town: Mendocino, Santa Cruz, Cotati, Hayward. We played for women's events: Health Collectives, Poetry Unions, Women's Day Celebrations, political benefits. At Provo Park in downtown Berkeley, we played at the "Nobody for President Rally" in 1976. Wavy Gravy was there and made jokes about nobody: Nobody knows, Nobody can do it better.

We had a standing gig at the West Dakota, a club on San Pablo Avenue in Berkeley. We were on the bill with other groups, sometimes a lesbian band, B B K Roche, or the Rhythm Bones, who were friends of ours.

One night at the West Dakota while we were playing, there was a power outage in the neighborhood and all of our power went off. Only the drums were heard playing, the other instruments were amplified and now silent. We noticed there was an acoustic piano on the stage, a lovely Steinway grand. I played that and we tried another song.

Without the guitar and bass our sound was greatly diminished so the singer, Lynn, tried something else. She organized the audience into two parts and had them singing rounds in harmony. I was impressed! This was in the midst of a long drought in the Bay Area. I remember that night very well; I loved the ingenuity of our band at entertaining the audience with no power, and when I got home and lay down in my bed I heard the welcome sound of rain!

The Ways of Meringue was playing a lot and making some money. We rehearsed and played gigs at night. Pinel was all day. I was starting to feel overwhelmed with work in both sectors of my life. I loved both of these jobs, but I was starting to think I should choose one and give it all my attention. At Pinel, Elizabeth was a student teacher who worked with me. I liked her very much. She was very capable and creative with the children who loved her dearly. I felt if I had the right replacement, I could leave Pinel with less worry and sadness.

Should I?

Nobody For President rally WOMB — Provo Park Berkeley 1976

1976

From my Journal:

January 1976
The year of the dragon coming up!
The Ways of Meringue on the rise!
Stay high with music
Sallie wrote a song, "Doing the Best I Can"
That's IT!   It's THAT!
Learning discipline is part of freedom-----
Yoga and body exercises a half hour a day
8 hours sleep
time alone, time to slow down
time alone, time to slow down
piano exercises, boogie-woogie each day
Keeping sex energy under control---no problem
When you replace it with rock'n roll!

We were busy with rehearsals and gigs. I continued to seek help to develop as a musician. I took classes at Laney College in Ear Training and Musicianship. Learning about chords was apropos, and I applied my understanding to the tunes in the band. Soloing eluded me. I had never messed around at the piano making things up; I was stuck on the melody of the song or on the chord changes. I had no experience or understanding of improvisation. That came later when I studied and played jazz.

Debbie, the guitarist in Ways of Meringue, was the star of the group. She shone brightly in her playing. Surprisingly to me, she had a rather dour side to her personality. I was amazed that someone with such musical ability, someone who could take us listeners and dancers to such heightened states and joyful feelings with her playing, was not a satisfied and totally happy person. Debbie and Maureen were a couple: Maureen, a positive and happy person provided Debbie with a strong, constructive point of view. Lorraine, the drummer and songwriter, had a melancholy and sometimes-gloomy attitude like Debbie, but both of these women could be silly and funny at times. Marcia, Lorraine's partner, was a stabilizing force.

My heart was torn in two: I wanted to stay at Pinel; I adored the children, the land, the job of being creative as a teacher. I also wanted to pursue my dreams of being a musician in a band. I had a beautiful dream of playing an organ in a tree in the woods. In the tree behind me a door opens, and I see a cave going deeply down into the roots of the tree. There's light, sparkling, beckoning me. But I'm afraid to go down because the door might close.

I feel like I'm searching for the music. In another dream, I'm playing the piano and blood appears on the keys. I wanted the music very much, but this was the unknown, the road not traveled. I had always had a "day" job, and that was the important work, the work that sustained me. Economically I was unsure that I could support myself with music. I was thirty-six years old.

I had a connection for buying pot on my street: my dear friend and neighbor, Marty. He had excellent weed, good organic Mexican lids (ounces) for cheap. Friends of mine, some also on the same street, asked me to score for them. I did. One day Marty said to me, "Why don't you buy a pound and deal it to your friends. You're doing them a favor. Why not make a little bread on the side for yourself?" What a good idea. I bought a balance scale and plastic baggies and set up shop in my kitchen closet. At first I just dealt to my close friends in the neighborhood. Then I expanded little by little over a period of years and had a thriving cottage industry.

At Pinel I made $400 a month and had Kaiser health insurance. With Ways of Meringue, I made about $200 a month, and now I had a little more on the side with my closet business.

My rent and expenses were low; I rarely had to go to the doctor. The financial side of leaving Pinel seemed brighter now, and I trusted the Great Goddess to take care of me.

I made lists of the positives and the negatives of leaving my job that I loved. I had to figure this out soon. It was spring now and Alice was talking about next year at the school. I needed to talk to Elizabeth, my student teacher, and see if she was interested in taking my place. She was. That was a relief. The organ dream also seemed to point in the direction of music. I seemed to have made up my mind.

I wanted to do something big for the children before I left. I had told no one yet. I asked the older kids about putting on a play, namely The Wizard of Oz. They got very excited and started casting the roles immediately. Frederick would be the Lion; he had the lion costume he wore every Halloween. Dov would be the Tin Man, Heather the Scarecrow. But who would be Dorothy? Lisa and Sharon B. were the contenders. I went to Sharon and said, "The other best part is the Wicked Witch. If you did that you would paint your face green and jump down from the cubbies onto the stage and scare everyone with your cackling laugh!" Sharon wanted to do that, so Lisa took on Dorothy. Morgan was about seven and he piped up, "I'll be Toto!" The little children, five and six, would be the Munchkins and the Monkeys. The Wizard was claimed by Greg, and the Good Witches came forth. Wow! This was sure to be a hit!

I knew the book by Frank Baum and the children knew the movie. First I wrote a script but soon scrapped that for the way the children wanted to do it. We had rehearsals and sang the song, "Over the Rainbow." Soon everyone at the school was involved. A giant carton appeared, to be painted as Dorothy's house. Someone set up curtains to be pulled back and forth on the stage. The parents offered to be the costume providers and the face painters. Although I was the official "director," the children mainly directed themselves, and I loved watching them figure out how to stage the show.

I talked to the WOMB* and told them my plan of leaving my teaching job. Then I asked them to play at the school the day of the play. Act One, the Wizard of Oz. Act Two, the Ways of Meringue. They agreed to play for free.

May 2nd was the Sunday of the Big Show. I sat in front of the stage on the floor, but I didn't have to direct or cue anyone; they astounded me. These young actors got thoroughly into character. They added emotional content I had not seen in rehearsals. When the Wizard directed Dorothy and her three companions to seek out the Wicked Witch and kill her, they all turned away and trudged off, drooping their shoulders with the burden of the job. Sharon, playing the Wicked Witch, let go a

* WOMB. Ways of Meringue Band

Wizard of Oz, Pinel
From left: Morgan, Frederick, Lisa, Dov — 1976

piercing shriek when they killed her. When the Wizard was unmasked he fell backwards. The song, *Over the Rainbow,* was sung with such feeling and beauty.

Many of my friends came to the performance and all the parents at the school were there. The applause was tremendous. The children were ecstatic. I was too. And then out came the electric instruments and the drums and the Ways of Meringue serenaded the crowd outside. What a day it was!

I had been consulting the *I Ching* all along in my struggle to make a decision. When I got the reading: "Before Completion, bringing order out of disorder," I knew I would tell Alice and Ray I was leaving. Elizabeth was ready to take over the little kids for me. They accepted my resignation with disappointment.

Now my journal is filled with sadness. After receiving the I Ching Reading of "Dispersion,"

I wrote:

Oh the pain of parting from pinel
Mother of mine
6 acres of mommy.........
and the children
their bodies
their laughs
their cries
their fights
their joyous play
the chase sallie game panting,
throbbing, hugging me all in a pile at the end
oh my dearest ones.

It was painful to separate, to change, to embark on something new. But now I knew it was the right thing for me. It was my childhood dream to devote myself to music. Mother sent a letter replying to mine about my decision to leave Pinel and follow a music career. She approved of my new "field!"

My journal proclaimed:

Music is my mistress now
Let me serve her well
Let me learn her ways
Let me play her songs
Let me find a way to say
I LOVE LIFE

WOMB
From Left: Sallie, Debbie, Lynn, Lorraine, Maureen — 1976

Changes, Changes, Changes

In the fall of 1976, I grieved a lot for my lost job at Pinel. I had left voluntarily, but I had to suffer the loss of a community of children and adults I had known for eight years. I knew the dates of the opening day that fall, the camping trip, the return. I felt bereft, but I busied myself with music: I listened, I studied, I practiced. The Ways of Meringue (WOMB) rehearsed, and played gigs.

Then I started going to Pinel once every few weeks to do a class for the older kids. We did music, and dancing in the Big Room with African drum records and Stevie Wonder. With the older girls, I did a project of looking through magazines of the day to find pictures of girls and women engaged in physical activity other than cooking and cleaning. To our amazement the only ad that showed women running or playing sports was for Tampax! Everything else was childcare or housework. I think the girls got the point: their role in society was defined and limited to bringing up children and keeping the house clean.

These excursions to Pinel were very satisfying to me. I was still a part of that community, and my sadness was assuaged.

The band was very active; we had jobs and interviews for local newspapers and women's journals. In one interview I said, "I think women are more supportive, less competitive, more cooperative and easier for me to understand. There are fewer underground, ulterior, sexual implications." Lorraine piped up,"Ya wanna bet?" We all laughed. For our New Years Eve gig, the newspaper, the Bay Guardian listed us: "Ways of Meringue at Bishop's

Coffee House. Promises to be an outrageous night of glitter and funk."

We were in the Gay Pride Parade, on a float in the parade, and on the stage in the park. There were thousands of people there. I was scared to death! Maureen instructed me, "Don't look at the crowd; focus on the band and the music." Good advice.

We had a Halloween gig at a fancy hotel. We wore tuxedo tee shirts, pants, beards, moustaches and Lynn, the singer, dressed as a suburban housewife. A gay men's band played also. I loved their campy version of "It's So Nice to Have a Man Around the House."

There was a cocaine dealer in our band. At most gigs we were treated to a line on our break. It was like candy to me, sweet but unnecessary. I had had experience seeing people overuse cocaine and wreck their lives. A little coke once in a while made things sharp and clear and you could get a boost of energy, but too much made you paranoid, fearful, and anti-social. Inevitably having a dealer in the band caused conflicts. People imagined slights to their egos; people wanted more cocaine. I steered clear of that. After a year, Lynn, the singer, left the band and was replaced by Terry, a singer we knew from another local band. Big changes. Debbie left Maureen for a relationship with Terry. Marcia left Lorraine. This shook the band like an earthquake. Maureen started a relationship with Lorraine who was now abusing drugs in her depression. These shifts were not conducive to playing music harmoniously. The end was in sight and tension was heightened by using cocaine. I was not happy. I didn't want to participate when people were going over the edge. The joy of playing was poisoned by jealousy, resentment, and other bad feelings.

Bands are like families. You come together with love; you feel warm, secure, satisfied. The initial stages can be intoxicating and thrilling. As time goes on people change and maybe dissension and disagreements arise. If drugs are present, these conflicts are amplified. You hang on to what you had, but you really don't have it anymore. Eventually you let go. It's best to move on. The Ways of Meringue broke up.

Towards the end of Ways of Meringue Band, another momentous change was coming in my personal life. My precious kitty, Krishna Murphy, was sick and nearing the end of his life on earth. When the vet said, "Now we need to use an IV drip," I said. "No. Now it's time to go home and rest and prepare." I fed Krishna baby food on a spoon until he refused the offer. I had him on a plumpy cushion in the bedroom closet, away from Lucifer, my other kitty. I meditated and communed with him every minute I could. After four days, he passed with me at his side. I had my hands pressed together in prayer fashion, and they suddenly flew open on their own. I looked at Krishna and saw he was gone. My heart broke and my tears gushed.

I wrote:

Krishna the cat so elegant so proud so magnificent
To the end his spirit his independence his self
So refined so right so elegant so magnificent
Take love take gentleness take

kindness   *take softness*

When you go to the cosmos

Come back again   *re-formed*

re-born   *re-newed*

My sweet angel cat

"Goodnight sweet prince and flights of angels sing thee to thy rest"

After Krishna passed two magical things happened. An orange kitty came to my back door, mewing to be let in. I had never seen this cat before, but I let him in. He stayed the night, then I never saw him again.

A few weeks after I had buried Krishna in the public strip outside my house, a tree started to grow. It grew and grew, a California White Oak tree, a native, but I saw no other in my neighborhood. I knew I had disturbed a seed long buried and at the same time it was a cosmic event to me. Vishnu, the preserver follows Krishna, the creator.

The universe moves in mysterious ways.

Small Time Dope Dealer

After WOMB broke up, my source of income was my closet business of selling ounces and half ounces of marijuana to a selected group of friends and acquaintances. Literally a closet business: my scale, baggies, and supplies were in my kitchen closet—a walk-in affair with shelves like a pantry. I never felt paranoid about the police. After all this was Berkeley; pot busting was a low priority for the cops, and I was very small time. I did however, feel that I needed to keep respectability in my house and neighborhood. My landlord, Mr. Palmer, lived downstairs, a lovely African-American man who would frown on such a business. My next-door neighbor, Mrs. Robinson, also African-American and a churchgoer, ran a day care center in her home. I was sure she would not approve.

I kept strict limits on my customers. Only a few people could come over each day and no one could leave the car running to come and go quickly. Everyone cooperated. We spent a little time chatting at the kitchen table so no suspicion could be aroused. I had a lot of friends and these were social calls. Ha!

Later WOMB became EBMUD (East Bay Mud). I started that latin/funk/rock band with friends. That band lasted four years. Finally, I reached my limit for amplified music and started to study jazz with Susan Muscarella at the UC Berkeley Jazz Ensembles. This was an exciting and challenging musical undertaking. The literature of jazz is vast and as deep as classical music and improvisation was a daunting prospect for me. You need all your wits about you if you want to play jazz, and I did. Fortunately for me smoking pot was an aid in this process. When I got high, I could focus on my tasks. I could get lost practicing beautiful piano voicings for chords and time did not exist. I started to familiarize myself with the Great American Songbook and particularly the compositions of Duke Ellington. My listening skills were enhanced, I thought, by being stoned. I could follow the piano through the intricacies of melodic improvisation on recordings. I felt spiritually uplifted as I did in my youth when I lay on the floor and luxuriated in Beethoven's symphonies.

This was the positive side of my life at the time, but there were negative aspects too. During the eleven years I dealt pot, I had a few unsettling experiences. I was conscious of being a small, single woman living alone in my apartment with a pound or two of weed in my closet. I took precautions about allowing men I didn't know into my circle. One woman friend vouched for her male friend with assurances that he was trustworthy and would never intimidate me. I said okay, he could have my number. On his second visit he carried a hardback book, "The Joy of Sex," prominently displayed under his arm and he verbally came on to me. I set him straight and sent him on his way. This experience affirmed my intuition that I should have only women buyers.

Another time a woman friend let my number slip to her boyfriend, who called me and made insinuations on the phone about my business. I called her right away and told her a made-up story that I was in trouble and no longer dealing. No problem cutting her off. She never called again.

I had a code for talking about pot on the phone: books. Paperbacks were cheap ounces, hardbacks were the expensive, select variety. People were creative with their questions. "I'd like to read a good novel, but I'm on a low budget."

"I want a book by a Nobel Prize Winner, the best you have."

I also had "shake," the much cheaper, less potent leaves of the marijuana plant, mostly composted in the process of cleaning the buds.

"I'm really scrabbling this week, do you have any used, torn books?"

When my mother visited me every so often, I closed up shop while she was with me. People mostly cooperated but occasionally someone called with a desperate plea for a book. I sneaked a bag of dope to them surreptitiously. My mother was shocked when I told her I smoked pot; she would have been appalled if she knew I was dealing. Once when she was in town, EBMUD had a gig in a backyard in my neighborhood. I invited Mom to come and gave her a heads up. "There will be people smoking pot," I advised her. "Well," she harrumphed, but she came to the party. Evidently someone passed her a joint, because the story she told most often when she returned to Norfolk, according to my brother, was: "I went to a party and someone offered me a marijuana cigarette."

I was ripped off once by a friend, who bought a pound of shake and promised to pay me the following week. It was foolish of me to trust him, but I had known him a long time. He lived in the neighborhood; he was also a musician, so I felt a kinship. He didn't. I never saw him again. Small loss.

I thought of my business as a community service.

People wanted to smoke; I had a good connection and ran a respectable establishment. After eleven years I started to think: Is this my career? Will I keep doing this job? No, I knew that was not the right path. I was a musician; I was a teacher; these were worthy occupations, dope dealing was not. I needed some help and a good friend recommended a therapist. Marija was a nurse as well as a therapist, and she was interested in psychic phenomena. She had me talk, and then she mirrored back my ideas and feelings. I saw my problem: I had not felt apprehensive or uptight about dealing, because I smoked pot every day, and that masked my negative feelings. I didn't admit to myself that I was not doing the right thing, since I got high daily and didn't look at that aspect. Pot is a mild intoxicant, but used every day for years, it does bury anxiety and stress.

I decided to stop smoking. My body was glad. I felt better and I had more energy and clearer thinking. Marija helped me work out the negativity, and I started to think of teaching children again. I needed a job, but one less demanding than Pinel or public school teaching. I needed time to continue studying and playing music. I sought a job at a nursery school and landed one at the Gay Austin School.* I didn't realize at first what a prestigious school it was. I was happy to be with children again; I loved these little ones. The director paid a good wage and the staff was friendly and welcoming. After a few months I did realize this was a very good job, and if I were found out to be dealing dope, I would lose it. So I closed up my closet business and returned to the straight and narrow working world with regular hours and IRS W2 forms.

* Named after the well-known early childhood educator Gay Austin.

I was still pursuing jazz, which was very fulfilling. I started to take a few students at the urging of my teacher. I made new friends at the nursery school. I didn't need any extra stimulant herbs, being with young children made me appreciate my own early childhood, which was blissful. I recognized the wisdom of my mother's early childhood training: unconditional love and positive discipline. I did my best to emulate that in my role as early childhood teacher.

EBMUD - PART ONE

After I left WOMB, I was looking for people to play with. Even though I felt not ready, unprepared, a neophyte, I loved the experience of jamming with other musicians, most of whom were more advanced than I. This was good for me, I learned a lot and it was daring and exciting.

My close friend Maud lived across the street from me, and she knew a whole group of people who played classical music. Stephen was part of that group. With flaming red hair and a cherub-like face, he smiled a lot. I found it ironic that he enjoyed music and people, he sang and played the flute, but his conversation and jokes were on the dark side. I discovered later that he was gay and being gay and out was hardly known in 1977.

Stephen played and sang in the early Baroque style, and he loved jazz and knew some rock songs. We jammed together in the jazz-rock style and had a good time. Someone asked us to play at a wedding, and we jumped at the chance. On their set list was "Bye Bye Blackbird." Later, Stephen remembered that when he sang that song, he was too young and inhibited to change the lyric from "she" to "he." When the line says "sugar is sweet and so is she," he sang "sugar is sweet and so is tea!"

The Starry Plough was our hangout, and we knew Rick, an excellent guitar player and Jerry a fine conga player and percussionist. Jerry was tall and good-looking and was always around to sit in with the various groups who played at the Plough. He added a lot to every group with his sharp sense of time and his colorful additions of cowbell, cabasa, and other percussion instruments. Jerry was in our band from start to finish. He and Rick joined me and Stephen at my house for some jamming.

Stephen had a friend, Nels, who played electric bass. He joined our group and we loved it. Now we were ready to play a gig. Conveniently, I helped out with the booking at the Plough and I set us up for every other Tuesday night. We were excited to have a band and a gig, now we needed a name. At one rehearsal I asked everyone their astrological sign. We were all earth and water. "That makes mud," I said. "East Bay Mud" quipped Jerry who was good with words and took a cue from the eponymous water company. "Yes," we all laughingly agreed. My artist friend Maud drew a flyer for us with a pail of mud at the beach to announce our gig. We were off and running.

Our repertoire was eclectic to say the least, from the rowdy rock song "Sea Cruise" to the elegant jazz classic "Satin Doll." "Girl From Ipanema" was a favorite, and we improvised two Latin tunes with Jerry leading the way on his congas and percussion toys. I was thrilled when Jerry gave me his old cowbell. I had passed the time/rhythm test!

We played "Sweet Georgia Brown" at breakneck speed and once Stephen missed the first word of the lyric, so he sang "blah blah blah" throughout. I'm sure no one but the band noticed this unusual scat singing.

One night someone tried to drive a car through the front door of the Plough. It made an extremely loud noise, but the band played on and nobody was hurt. One never knew what would happen next in this venue.

As the front person (the person in front of the band), Stephen had to deal with the folks who came up to the bandstand to comment, request a song, or gush. "You are so androgynous," effused a hippy girl one night, much to Stephen's chagrin. Some people, in their cups, would stagger up and try to sing along.

The band was attracting more and more people to the Plough on Tuesday nights; people piled in to dance and enjoy the music and the ambience we created. We made practically no money. We did it for the music and the high.

Our big virtuoso number was Chick Correa's "Spain." Stephen had notated the famous rhythm lick from that song and taught it to us. We did it a cappella with Jerry's cowbell. But now Stephen told us he was unhappy with his singing and flute playing. He thought it wasn't jazzy or funky enough, and he was leaving the band. I was very surprised and disappointed.

I had a friend, Jeffrey; we met through leftist political connections. He played trombone. Jeffrey was another tall, good-looking guy with a great sense of humor, a punster. He was a rent lawyer and activist. He liked the band and joined us, and brought in a friend, Richard who played sax. Now we had a horn section!

Kim was around the Plough and heard we were looking for a singer. He was a tall, willowy guy with longish locks of brown hair falling in his face. Kim sang and wrote songs. We invited him to a rehearsal and he fit right in. He and Jeffrey were Francophiles and became good friends.

The original Rick guitar player had moved on, and we had various other people sitting in. Rick A. came along and was agreeable to joining us. Rick had a wonderful dog named Ivan, a largish German Shepard mix, who we all loved. Rick also had a truck that was big enough to carry my equipment, so now we could play at other clubs. I had a Fender Rhodes piano, an amplifier and a

PA system I had acquired along the way. I didn't drive at the time. My dear Maud would drive me and my stuff down the street to the Plough for gigs. Now Rick was willing to take on that job. That was a godsend.

Our original bass player had also left—it was a round robin of players coming and going. Jerry and I were the only originals left, but what fun to play with so many different people. Rick knew Aron, who was a bass player interested in joining us. He was a bearded man with snappy clothes and an attitude. He was very sure of himself. He and Rick played well together although they were so different in appearance. Rick was a hippie with long, unkempt hair who wore tee shirts and jeans. A motley crew is what we were.

Big Bob joined us on the drum set, a large guy with long blonde hair. All of a sudden we were eight pieces and musicians loved to sit in with us. Will Scarlett was a terrific harmonica player who showed up with his suitcase of harmonicas and added his lyrical, rhythmical playing to our sound. This group was cooking, and we were elated to generate such good energy and have so many people dancing joyously in front of us.

Lovey Lovejoy was an African American sax player who often stopped in to play. His playing reflected his name of love and joy. We were thrilled to have such a good musician play with us. Everyone at the Plough was elevated and energized to have scintillating music in the air.

Our first gig away from our home base, the Starry Plough, was at the Berkeley Square, about two miles away. The Square was like a large living room; there were rugs on the floor and a fireplace in the middle of the section where we performed. The bar was along the side as you came in before you reached the music room. People sat in booths and at tables around the fireplace. At this time the Square was mostly a jazz venue, so we revved up our jazz repertoire. There was no dancing, but one night a friend of Jeffrey's roller-skated into the Square. He glided past the bar and up to the band that was not on an elevated stage. He knocked over the microphone and smacked into Jeffrey's trombone. This friend thought of his skating as a lark, but it was a disaster. Jeffrey had to have his instrument repaired.

Larry Blake's was a happening place on Telegraph near the campus, restaurant upstairs, bar and music downstairs. Students from the University made up the rousing and enthusiastic crowd of drinkers and dancers. There was no official dance floor; people danced pressing up against the band. Jeffrey had to stand on a table to avoid poking a dancer with his trombone slide.

Setting up the band in this venue seemed dangerous. Nothing ever happened, but we plugged our power strips into the main electrical outlet that was located on the sweaty, wooden beams near the ceiling. This small space had no window and little ventilation.

I was keeping up on the accompaniment side of playing and felt some pressure from the band to do more soloing. This was a dilemma for me, because I was uncomfortable trying to improvise. I solved the problem by composing a solo, memorizing it and playing it the same way every time. One night at the Square we were playing a blues and I played my usual, composed solo. Someone sitting in with us said, "I'd like to hear you play more, get loose and jam!" Right, I wanted to do that, but I didn't know enough about improvising at that point.

Indeed it was many years till I felt at ease improvising in front of people. I needed to study jazz.

I contributed a lot to the band on the business level. Jeffrey and I would call club owners and managers to try to set up auditions or at least get them to listen to a live tape. It was a hard and thankless job, since the other band members had no idea how to do this or how difficult it was. Managers were never "in." Setting up an appointment was a Kafkaesque task, for the manager never had time. How they lined up the music was a puzzle; no one was ever available to talk to. But we were persistent, and soon we had gigs at Larry Blake's, La Peña, Ashkenaz, and other venues. Ashkenaz was a particular favorite place. David Nadel, the owner and manager, was not like those other managers, and we hit it off right away. David was down to earth, accessible, politically active, and a dear person who loved to dance. The beautiful, large, wooden dance floor was perfect for our following of cavorting, creative dancers.

Jeffrey and I were political activists and everyone in the band was sympathetic to the left wing causes we supported. Our band played benefits galore: for the Berkeley Tenants Union, Women Refuge Centers, People aiding Nicaragua, The San Francisco Mime Troupe, Casa El Salvador, Grassroots newspaper and many more. It was very satisfying to support the movements we believed in, in a musical and pleasurable way.

Halloween 1979 was coming up, and we had a gig at the Starry Plough. I presented my idea for costumes to the seven men in the band. They would dress as an all-girl band, and I would be the sleazy manager with a cigar. They liked the idea but when the night arrived only four dressed as women; the other three couldn't handle dressing as a woman, but they did wear costumes. The guys who dressed as women really dolled it up. Kim, the singer, shaved his moustache, wore a pretty silky dress and flounced around. Aron, the bassist, powdered his beard and wore a stuffed bra under his housedress. The guitarist, Rick, had on a long slinky gown, and Jeffrey wore short shorts and nylons. What a kick! I wore men's clothes and put my long hair up under a man's hat. I carried a fake cigar and pinched the "girls'" butts. They acted submissive to me. We really hammed it up. One friend who came to most of our gigs said, "I was there, but I didn't see you"—the perfect disguise.

Top: Kim, Rick, Aron. *Bottom: Jerry, Sallie, Bob.*
— Halloween 1979

EAST BAY MUD - PART TWO

Bands are like onions, there are inner circles and outer circles. In Ways Of Meringue Band, I was in the outer circle, the last to join and not a lesbian as the core members were. That was fine with me. It was challenging enough just to play in the group and try to keep up with the musicianship of the others.

In EBMUD, I was in the inner circle: I had started the band and was instrumental in getting us the gig at the Starry Plough. EBMUD's inner circle was Jerry and I from the original band, Rick, the guitarist, Jeffrey, the trombonist, and Kim the singer. Jerry had been grumbling about the bass/drums rhythm section that we had; it wasn't funky enough; the drummer, Bob, didn't kick the bass drum; Aron didn't punch the bass line. Now we five had a discussion and even though we didn't want to hurt these individuals, it was a musical decision that for the band to progress we needed another rhythm section. Not only that, but we were aware of Richard, the sax player's limitations. He played out of tune sometimes and didn't listen properly to know when to play and when to lay out.

I was very conflicted; this was a family band. How could we fire our friends? Well, these three were not the best of friends. Aron had been acting arrogantly and insensitively lately and that annoyed people. Bob kept his distance from the band and seemed to know something was going to happen. Richard was oblivious and helped with the promotion of gigs. He would take it the hardest. Jeffrey said, "We are going to commit murder!" I wrote in my journal:

ambivalence and yet decision/ personalities and playing/ we want to change the bass and drums/ we want another sax player/ we don't want to hurt these 3/ it's a musical decision/ it's a difficult decision/ it's a sticky situation

Breaking up is so very hard to do/ How can we do this deed?/ How can we not do this deed?/ once said, done, something had to change/ it would have drifted away one way or another/ Now we reconstitute IT/rebuild it/renew it/ rejuvenate it/ in nature plants die and are reborn/ birth is painful for the mother and the child. Dis-band/ De-band/ un-band bandy about/ Reform/ Re join/Regain/ Remain

After agonizing over the problem for weeks, Jeffrey, Rick and I went to visit the three who were out of favor, separately at their homes. We told them the truth: it was a musical decision; we needed another bass/drums set up. To Richard, we said we wanted a more advanced jazz player. They were all surprised to say the least. Aron called me afterwards to say: "That was not a family-like thing to do," but he also said we could still be friends and do business together. He meant he would still buy pot from me and that was good! What a relief. Bob told a mutual friend he thought it was harsh to be cut out that way. Richard was depressed about it. I felt terrible, but the band had gigs and we carried on with bassists and drummers sitting in.

Ken, one of Jerry's roommates, joined us on sax and that was a big boost: he was an excellent player and blended in with us socially. I was inspired to write out horn arrangements for some of our songs, tenor sax on top, trombone part below. I was thrilled to hear Jeffrey and Ken play something I had written.

One drummer we all liked played some gigs with us and then went off to join a "new wave" band. Bob J. played bass with us for a time, a very capable and funky player who could slap his bass appropriately, but then he moved back east, and we had to look again. We played with many drummers and bassists who were terrific players, but they all had other projects, so we kept looking until we found Chip, a very strong bass player, a very nice person, and an African-American man. At last we had some diversity. We went through many drummers, some of whom were so loud I was discouraged, but finally we landed Angel, a large and smiling Hispanic guy who knew how to kick the bass drum and got along well with us. He was, thankfully, not the loudest drummer we interviewed. More diversity was welcome.

Just when it seemed we were all set, Rick, the guitarist announced he was leaving town. Ah, I knew what that meant for me: I would have to learn to drive and buy a vehicle. Rick had a large truck, and he took me and my equipment to the gigs. My mother was thrilled at the news of me learning to drive. She had never taken that on and wanted her daughter to accomplish that task. Mother paid for four driving lessons, and a friend took me to a deserted parking lot to practice on her VW bug, an automatic transmission car. After three lessons, my driving teacher tricked me; he said as I was driving on Claremont Avenue: "Now turn left." That was a line the Department of Motor Vehicle's line for driving tests. I passed as he said I would.

Now there was another hurdle to be surmounted. I knew what kind of vehicle I would like to buy: a Datsun pick-up truck. I had seen another piano player driving her little Datsun around with her equipment in the back. It looked perfect to me. The problem was that it was a standard transmission car, and now I needed to learn to use a stick shift.

Another woman friend offered to help me in exchange for music lessons. I felt so fortunate that people were helping me with what I needed. I had a hard time at first with the shifting until a neighbor of mine said, “It’s a physical response.” Well that made it easier for me. I loved physical activity; I danced, I exercised, I played games with children, so yes, I could learn to shift gears, and I did.

My mother was so impressed with my progress that she sent me $2000 to purchase a truck. I bought “Sapphire” from a woman who was happy to sell it to me. My friend Brian came with me to check it out, and he told me it was a good car. “Don’t you want to drive it?” asked Joan, the seller, as Brian sat behind the wheel after we concluded the business. “Oh yes, I will,” I replied, but I still had a few more lessons before I felt comfortable. Driving at night was a challenge. I remember the first time I said to Sandy, my teacher, “You must be kidding.”

“You get used to it,” she answered.

I did and I learned to drive on the freeway as well. I realized I liked to drive; it gave me confidence and a great feeling of independence. My graduation was driving Sandy to Stinson Beach to visit my friends there. It was difficult, but I succeeded.

In the meantime we had been searching for a new guitarist. Tony was discovered—a wonderful player, a composer and a compatible band-mate! For me, he was all of those things, but he also played incredibly loud. Each time he started his solo, I practically fell off my

Sallie — EMBUD 1978

piano bench. He was melodic in his improvisations but with such a piercing sound that I couldn't enjoy it. I was starting to wake up in the morning after a gig with my ears ringing. Not only was the guitar loud, but also the two drummers, the trap drums and the conga drum amped up everyone's volume. I was very uncomfortable with that. I realized that I wanted to play a gentler music, more acoustic, less electric music: jazz. I started taking piano lessons with Susan Muscarella at the UC Berkeley jazz ensembles. It was just what I wanted.

EBMUD played on, more popular than ever with our new personnel. We played every weekend at Ashkenaz, La Peña, the Starry Plough, and other places, sometimes twice a weekend. Occasionally we had a gig in San Francisco. I remember one such gig where some man in the club took offense at Jerry's attitude, his looks or something, and this belligerent came up to the stage and tried to punch Jerry. Pandemonium ensued. I crept under my piano until the fracas was over, and we never did find out why we were attacked.

Once we played a gig on a houseboat in Sausalito and another time we went to Chico for a college dance. I was amazed at what happened on these gigs away from our home turf where most of the guys had girlfriends. Young women sidled up to the men in our group and seduced them. These young women were irresistible to our band mates; they followed the flow of sexual attraction with these lovely young groupies.

Now it was 1981, and Jeffrey and Kim announced that they were leaving on trips: Kim to France, Jeffrey to India with his new wife Laura. This was my chance to leave as well. I was unwilling to do the business of the band without Jeffrey and the volume of the band was disturbing my peace! So I declared that I too would leave. Jeffrey, Kim and I discussed this and we decided that the name "EBMUD" would be dissolved on our departure. We knew another dance band would form on our heels and it did: "Backbone" was Jerry's creation and it lasted a few months.

In February we told our friends that our last gig would be in June at Ashkenaz, a benefit for Grassroots, a leftie newspaper. Thus began the countdown. As we approached the deadline our posters proclaimed, "Only five gigs left." We had a mailing list that I handled, and we postered up the neighborhood and Telegraph Avenue.

Finally the night arrived, and Ashkenaz was packed with hundreds of people, our friends, our families, our dancers. We were exuberant, and I was especially happy

Halloween, EBMUD, Ken, Bob, Jerry, Kim, Sallie, Jeffrey — Ashkenaz 1980

that since my jazz lessons had begun, I had improved a lot and improvising was becoming easier. We listened to the tape of our performance the Ashkenaz sound people had made as we packed up our instruments. When my solo on "You are the Sunshine of My Life," came on it sounded good! I said to Jerry, "Is this me?"

"You only wish," he said ironically, smiling. It was.

Postscript: Three years later in 1984, we had a reunion gig, again at Ashkenaz...two hundred or so people were there, ecstatic at our reappearance on the scene. It was a glorious night, and I was once again thrilled that my study of jazz was enhancing my playing. We all had a good time but we knew it was over; we were on separate paths now and EBMUD was an unforgettable memory.

Apparently our dancers and followers remembered too. Up until around 2011, thirty years after we ended, people would come up to me at the Berkeley Bowl or on the street and ask, "Weren't you in a band?"

Epilogue - Moving On

When EBMUD was over, when the ringing in my ears ceased, a new space opened up in my mind. More time! I could spend the time playing the lovely exercises my teacher, Susan Muscarella, gave me. Susan was the head of the University of California at Berkeley Jazz Ensembles. She was and is a very giving, generous person. She assigned me to play in casual jazz combos around the campus. Her crowning gift to me was recommending me to the UC Alumni Jazz Big Band when they needed a pianist. John Coppola was the musical director of that aggregate. Johnny had played trumpet with the Woody Herman Jazz Orchestra for twenty years. He was very knowledgeable. I paid close attention when he instructed the trumpets, trombones, and saxes how to swing the beat. There were Count Basie piano solos written out in some charts—grist for my mill.

Susan also advised me to start teaching and that shocked me. I didn't feel qualified for that. Then I realized that there were people out there who knew less about jazz music than I did, and I could help them. My next career was launched! I studied Boogie Woogie piano on my own to have fun and to add to my teaching repertoire.

So another musical adventure was evolving. It was thrilling and fulfilling. But that's another story for another time.

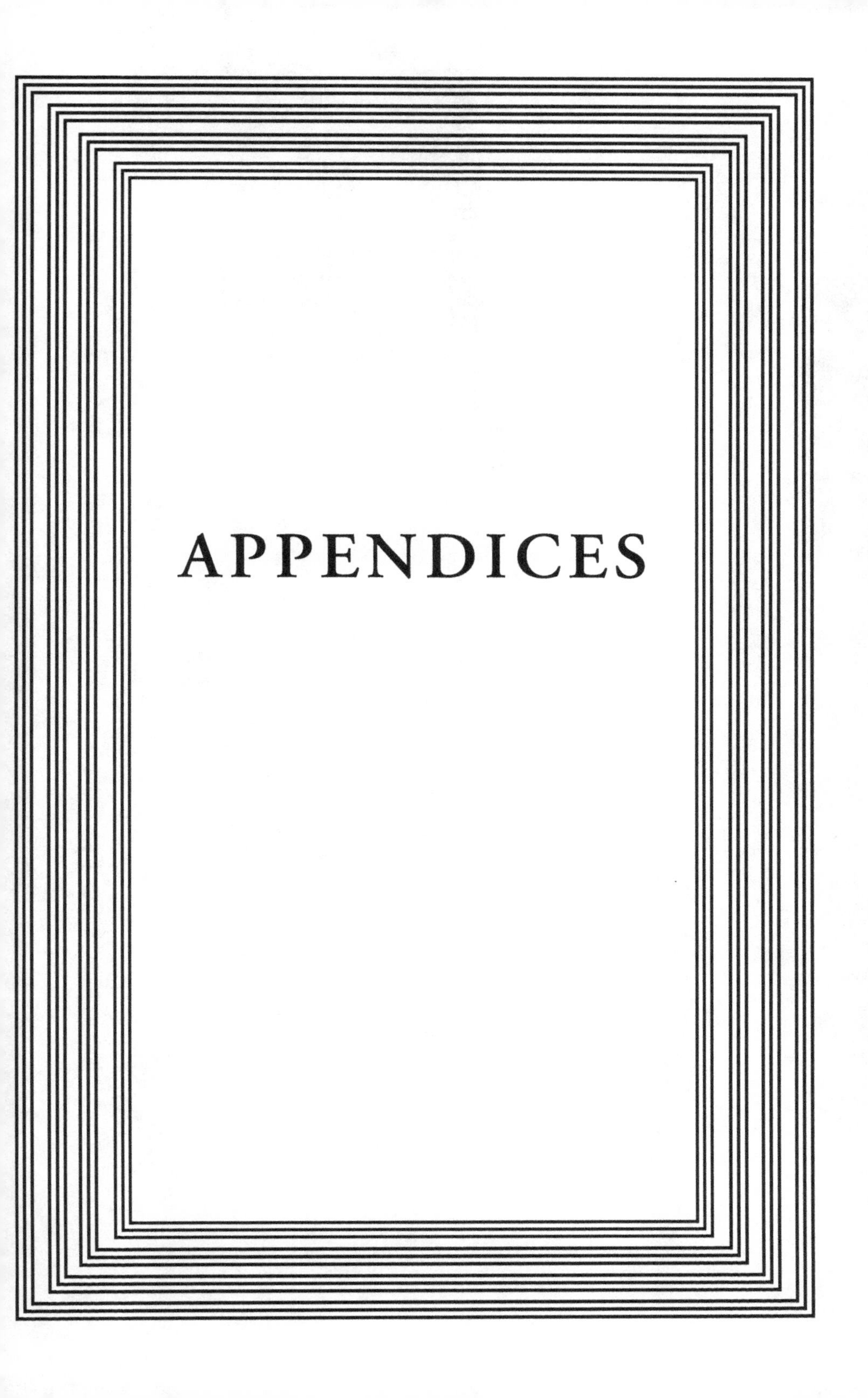

APPENDICES

Mother

Mother was a small woman, 5'2" at the most, but she was a large presence in our childhood. Being a stay-at-home mom, she directed our daily lives. Dad was involved with his children: he read to us, he played with us, he took us to visit his Southern relatives where we rode horses. But he was a workingman and sadly, more and more a drinking man as he aged. When I was eight or nine, I remember him sitting bent over the edge of his bed in the evening moaning, "I am a failure." He had less and less positive, upbeat energy as he got older. Mother never lost her zest for life or her zeal in directing her children's lives. She taught us how to behave. Her authority was ingrained and she used her authoritative voice to discipline us. That voice was not to be breached. We may have been spanked now and then but her jurisdiction was in her manner and her commands.

Mother's love for us was evident, not touchy-feely, but unconditional nonetheless. She grew more powerful as she grew older and Dad weakened. Mother did not allow failure. She not only survived, she triumphed! When she was in her 70s, I once tried to convince her to stay home from a symphony date when she had a bad cold. "My dear," she intoned, "I'm invincible!" She went to the concert and suffered no untoward consequences.

In her mind, Mother was a traditional wife and mother; she needed no liberation. She always found time to be involved with the schools we attended, to go to meetings at our church and to be active in the neighborhood association. Daddy never accompanied her to these meetings and events, she went on her own. There were other women whose husbands also stayed home with the children. These women friends supported each other.

Teenage issues were hard for Mother to deal with. She tried to tell me about sex and menstruation when I was twelve, but I was alienated by then and said, "Oh I know all that." I didn't, but she never tried again. I still obeyed her dictums, but I was more and more on my own in high school and in my social life with the neighborhood crowd as I grew up. At thirteen, I entered Bay Ridge High School, a few stops away on the subway. The nearby high school was Manual Training where girls learned secretarial skills and boys learned trades. There was little discussion about where I would go. I wanted an academic school. The principal of Bay Ridge was a woman my mother admired. Mrs. Fitzpatrick was a no-nonsense, old-fashioned person with a lacey handkerchief in the breast pocket of her jacket. She ran the school with precision and attention to detail. In 1952 this was an all-girl public school; academic standards were high and all students were expected and encouraged to study hard.

Jean Hanna, my mother, was born in Glasgow, Scotland in 1905. She never told anyone her age and even lopped off a few years on my brother Bill's birth certificate. It was a surprise to my brothers and me when a cousin on my father's side published a genealogical book of our family in 1985 and revealed that Mother was eighty years old. I never could get past seventy-five in my estimations, Mother had so much energy; she was healthy and was so sure of herself.

I have a picture of Mother when she was in high school in Scotland. She is smiling broadly and holding her hockey stick, dressed in a uniform with her

Mother in Scotland — 1922

classmates on the hockey field. Mother was one of the middle children of five siblings, two brothers and two sisters. Her mother, Ann Hanna, was from England, and her father hailed from Belfast, Ireland. Grandfather died when the children were young, and his family in Belfast invited my grandmother to Ireland to live with them. My grandmother packed up her five children and they took a train and a boat to Ireland. Within a few months my grandmother was uncomfortable as her in-laws were attempting to take over the raising of her children. She repacked and brought her brood back to Glasgow.

Mother did very well in school and earned a primary teaching certificate at age twenty-one. Since teaching jobs were hard to find then she hired herself out as a governess to a family that traveled. Maybe that's what spurred her to travel to New York City in the late 1920s. She got her green card in 1929. Her teaching certificate was not accepted in New York so she got a job as a receptionist in a doctor's office.

News that her mother had died came from Mother's sister in Scotland. This was devastating, Mother idolized her mother, "I couldn't understand how the sun could shine when my mother had died," she told us. After the funeral in Glasgow Mother returned to New York City.

Mother met my father and a group of young people who lived in Brooklyn Heights, a neighborhood in Brooklyn that bordered on the bohemian. The group of friends were intellectually curious about art, music and politics. Pictures of Mother at this time show a lovely, stylish woman who wore hats and posed pertly for photos. Daddy and his sister Janet were in this group as well as Larry Kennison who later became a math professor at Brooklyn College where I went to school. Larry and Mother had gone on some dates before she got together with Dad. The group of friends were well-read. Dad had a year of college at Mississippi State College. Most professed liberal political views except for Aunt Janet who was a staunch Southern conservative with typical Southern prejudices. Mother told a story of going to a meeting and at the end the speaker exclaimed, "Viva la Causa!" Mom didn't remember the cause, but she was impressed with the speaker's enthusiasm and the sound of the Spanish language.

Looking back I am amazed that Mother and Daddy's bookcase contained works by Havelock Ellis, a British physician who wrote about human sexuality. He accepted homosexuality as normal human behavior and inspired writers such as Radclyff Hall to write about it. I read "The Well of Loneliness," written by Hall out of that bookcase as a teenager. I couldn't figure out what it was about except that the heroine (a lesbian) was not accepted or respected by others. I had no idea what "lesbian" meant, and I'm sure the word was not used in the book, or I would have looked it up in the dictionary.

It was a goal of my mother to meet interesting people and people who were from other ethnic groups or races or those whose ideas varied from the norm. Mr. Faust was a church choir member and a follower of Henry George, a political thinker and writer who believed in a land tax to fund the government. Mother invited him to dinner a lot. He spiced up the conversations. When Mom got the news on the neighborhood grapevine that a Jewish family had moved into the neighborhood she sprang into action. She arranged for us, her children and herself to meet the new family. Marsha Abrams was my age and Alison, her sister, was a few years younger. Marsha and I were ten or eleven years old and we liked each other. We decided to have an after school club for us and younger children. We played inside games and usually bested our playmates. The club had dues, a nickel a time. After some weeks Marsha and I disbanded the club and absconded with the treasury. We went to the soda parlor and with our seventy cents we each had a "Special Treat," a sundae served in a tall glass. We didn't feel guilty; we enjoyed our sundaes! Marsha and I also organized a benefit party at my house for the March of Dimes. Mother saved the certificate I received for that. We raised $10, which we did not embezzle.

There was a blind woman in our neighborhood, Louise. Mother befriended her. Louise played Bridge with Braille cards, so Mother invited her to the Bridge parties at our house. Louise was a social worker and needed to keep up with the new findings in her field so Mother read to her. I took over that job at a certain point because Mother wanted me to have that experience. Mother knew another woman in our neighborhood who was French. Mom delighted in speaking French to this woman when they met on the street. This woman was a dwarf and stood about three feet tall. Mother never condescended to her and therefore neither did we. There was a knitting group in our neighborhood that met weekly, rotating houses to knit and talk. They called themselves "The Knitwits." I'm sure Mother thought of the name. I loved to fall asleep to the clicking of their needles and their laughing and palaver when they came to our home.

At church, Prospect Heights Presbyterian, Mother was active in many ways. She sang in the adult choir, a very musical mezzo-soprano, and she directed the Angel Choir, the young children's group. My brother Bill remembers her tapping out the time on her hymnal and expecting the children to watch her, stand tall, and sing well. Mother was in the Ladies Auxiliary and helped direct the Girl Scouts. She did not insist that I join the latter. I tried it but was not interested. Mother organized and directed "The Juvenile Frolics" for a few years. This was a musical revue: young children singing and dancing and cavorting about the stage. The most memorable performance for our family was my brother Billy singing in his enthusiastic, slightly out of tune voice, "Never Smile at a Crocodile." His baseball outfit was not buttoned properly at the fly and that was part of the charm.

In 1952 when I was thirteen, Mother and Daddy sang and danced in a Minstrel Show at the church. They wore blackface. This is shocking in today's culture but then there was no controversy. Although Mom and Dad were on the side of black people in their struggle to be equal, at this time, in the working class consciousness of our community, the minstrel show was paying tribute to the musicality and wit of the Negro race. I was mortified to hear Mother sing "A Good Man is Hard to Find" in a gravelly, bluesy way. I didn't want my proper mother to be sexy. Now I say "Bravo Mother!" for her chutzpah. Daddy sang "The Darktown Strutters Ball."

Music was such a part of my childhood. Thanks to my parents I was exposed to singing in church, singing at home at Christmas time, to listening to my Aunt Janet sing and play the piano all year round. I had piano lessons. We listened to music on the radio and when I was seventeen, I received a Victrola, a phonograph, so I could listen to the classical music I loved and the Rhythm and Blues hits of the day.

When I turned thirty-five in 1974, for some reason I decided to drop the recalcitrant feeling I had towards my mother. I was no longer a teenager, maybe I wanted to put away childish things, not to reveal the truth about my doings with sex and drugs, but to eliminate the conscious opposition I had towards my mother's traditional values. When she was coming to visit me in Berkeley, I removed a poem I had posted on my refrigerator because it had the word "fuck" in it. I wanted to celebrate Mother, not aggravate her. I hosted a Mother's Day party and invited friends to come and bring their mothers. She

Sallie and Mother — Deakin Street 1974

liked that. I had the popular bumper sticker "Love Your Mother" with a picture of the earth on my truck. She approved of that.

In the following years, I realized that giving up my rebellion against my mother had been good for my unconscious mind. It had opened up other channels in me, channels that allowed music to grow and develop. I told Mother this and she was pleased. However, Mother was still able to press those old buttons of mine in her words to me. But I didn't pursue that line of thinking. I would say, "Mom you know we disagree on that, let's talk of something else." If I were driving she would say, "Yes, dear, you're right." Now that was a huge concession to me.

Once when my two brothers and I were with Mother, we had an argument about something. There were four very different and strong opinions on the table. Mother suggested: "Why don't you say 'yes, mother" and then do what you want." She could no longer direct our lives, but she wanted the semblance of maternal authority.

The greatest gift Mother gave me was her optimistic and constructive outlook on life. Despite Daddy's alcoholism, which included verbal and at least one physical abuse that I witnessed, she maintained her love of life, her ability to rebound, her forgiving nature.

In my life I endured a terrible marriage to a drug addict/alcoholic. Luckily I was able to leave him after five years and no children, and creative a positive and happy life for myself. I credit Mother with her resilience and unwavering optimism for that. I gravitated to music and children because she too was drawn by those life-affirming elements. When I find myself in a rough patch, I don't give in to negativity but shore myself up to overcome adversity and return to a peaceful equilibrium.

Thank you dear Mother.

Sallie and Mother — Yosemite 1979

Daddy

My dad and I were very close in the early days. I adored him and he, me. I loved my mother too; there was no competition. We were a happy family. But Daddy's drinking worsened over the years; I still loved him, but I no longer adored him. I remember when I was eight or nine years old standing in the street on my skates, waiting for him to turn the corner onto our block when he was coming home from work. I was hoping he would be sober and not weaving along in an alcoholic haze. All the men and teenage boys in our community drank, but that didn't lessen the pain for me about my own dear daddy.

While I'm first generation American on my mother's side, I'm many generations American on my dad's side. Jacob Rhine (Rhyne, Rein) arrived here in 1768 from the German-Dutch area of Europe. My first cousin John Rison was very interested in genealogy and pursued the subject with our Aunt Janet, Dad's sister. Janet was very keen on adding to her prestige as a blue blood. She was a DAR member and exceedingly proud of her heritage. My dad must have felt something about his family's long history in this country, but he was more involved in his difficult childhood to pay it much mind. He had yearned for a close relationship with his father, which never happened.

Daddy was the 16th of 17 children of Drury Willoughby Rhyne, who was married twice. Mary, the first wife, died in her thirties after birthing nine children;, eight survived. Sarah Rebecca, the second wife, my grandmother lived to be 49 after raising nine of her own children plus the youngest of the first family. My

My handsome,charming Dad — 1947

Dad was nine when his mother died in 1913. His older sisters took care of him and Uncle Pete, the youngest child. The older sisters must have been very kind and loving, as the family bonds were close and strong.

Grandfather had a stint in the Civil War as a Confederate. He was fifteen when he tried to enlist and eighteen when he was accepted. He was wounded in Atlanta. In the family lore, he was sent home by an older soldier who put him on a horse, slapped the rump of the horse and said, "Ride like hell, kid." What really happened was he was in a hospital in Atlanta until he recovered. D.W. became a cotton farmer and eventually the Postmaster General of Lexington, Mississippi where he made his home, married and raised his children. Lexington was and still is a very small farming town, its main claim to fame being that it is the county seat of Holmes County, the poorest county in Mississippi, hence the country.

Granddad had a drinking problem. He went to New Orleans to sell his cotton and binge with his buddies. This did not further his career; he lost the Postmaster General job and had to sell some of his land to pay bills. When he was older and most of the children gone, the large home on "Rhyne Hill" dramatically burned to the ground. Later, Grandfather died in 1926 at age 80 with not a lot of family around him. My father was in New York City at the time and forever felt guilty about not being with his father when he died.

Grandfather was a Southern patriarch who loved his children and disciplined them harshly at times. The kids had to cut their own switches from the willow tree when a serious infraction was committed. He did not have a close relationship with any of his progeny, there were so many of them, and he was distracted by his drinking problem and his pressing business failures. Nonetheless, he had a soft heart, and his blustering was not always punitive. Daddy loved to tell the story of dinnertime at the large rectangular table with his father at the head. It was noisy at dinner with so many children jabbering and teasing each other. When Granddad had had enough he would rise from his seat and declaim, "Oh dry up and eat your dinner!" The children quieted down at once and got to the business of eating.

Growing up on a farm was ideal for children: they played outside, they ran, they explored the woods. The bonds between his siblings and my dad were solid and Dad kept in touch with them all through our childhood. Aunt Janet was a frequent visitor to our home in Brooklyn. She and Dad had come to New York City together in the 1920s. We saw a lot of Uncle Pete and his family when we were growing up. Pete was Dad's younger brother. He worked for Old Gold cigarettes and Dad and Pete shared the dubious habits of smoking and drinking. An older brother, Arch, had a wooden leg either from a WWI war wound or a train accident when he rode the rails after the war. Both stories were told over the years. Arch would take his wooden leg off when he visited us and prop it up on the couch. There was a hole in the knee joint of that prosthetic and he would crack nuts in that hole. Arch told my brother Bill that there was a snake in the wooden leg that would bite him if he put his hand inside it. We children were mesmerized.

Another older brother, Dan, was an accountant who was diagnosed with tuberculosis. After surgery to remove one lung, his doctor advised him not to work inside anymore. He would recover and live longer if he lived in the country and breathed fresh air. So Dan moved to Star, Mississippi, a tiny hamlet many miles from a city. I remember visiting Dan with my family one summer. We drove off the main highway onto a smaller road, then a smaller country lane, then onto a dirt road bumpy with ruts and gravel. Finally there was no road at all; we had to stop and park. In front of us was a tall, thick stand of corn. We all had to wiggle our way through the tall corn. My child mind must have wondered, "What was on the other side of this corn forest? Would it be the Land of Oz?" Well, no it was not that exotic, but it was a world away from our apartment house in Brooklyn. Dan's wood frame house was open to all, including chickens that strayed around with the air of ownership. A mule wandered up to the porch and Dan threw a blanket over his back so my brother Fred could ride him. My brother Bill remembers firing a shotgun in the yard. Dan lived until he was eighty-two in his country paradise.

It was a great pleasure to visit Dad's older sister, Adalene, Aunt Nene. She had married Thompson Kelly, a wealthy rancher who raised cattle for the Armour Meat Company. They lived in an old Southern mansion in Jeff, Alabama, a small community outside Huntsville. We got to ride horses and eat the scrumptious food at the formal dining table. The Kellys had a cook, a genial black woman who made the delicious food. At breakfast the table was laden with morning food: eggs, toast, oatmeal, pancakes, marmalade and jam, butter and maple syrup. In addition there was fresh fish, probably catfish. I loved it. I was a girl with a high metabolism like my Dad. We could eat big meals without consequences; we

Fred, Daddy and Billy, Sallie, Jeff — Alabama 1948

burned our calories quickly. We rode horses and swam in the neighbor's pool in the morning before the afternoon heat and humidity curtailed activity.

The house Nene and Thompson lived in was a colonial style Southern mansion with tall white columns on the porch. A long driveway bordered by hedges led up to the two-story home. There were many rooms on both floors, everything kept impeccably clean and uncluttered. Fans circulated the air; lighting was low to keep the house cool. We always visited in the summer. Outside was a slave cabin, kept unrestored for historical reasons. It was a pitiful small wooden shack where people must have been crowded in to serve the masters of the manor.

Uncle Thompson was the patriarch of the home and the community of Jeff. He was an old-fashioned man who was in charge of his domain. He was a kind man, respected by the black and white people in Jeff. He was very different from my dad. My brother Fred tells a story about Thompson that illustrates the differences. One summer when we were there we brought Rebel, our small fox terrier dog with us. Rebel had been Aunt Janet's dog and he was named for the Confederates. Uncle Thompson did not allow dogs in the house overnight. Rebel had to be in the outdoor kennel with the other dogs. Thompson also did not allow brothers and sisters to sleep in the same bedroom. (Did he know that Fred, Billy and I slept in the same bedroom till I was seventeen?) I slept upstairs in Thompson's house with my mother and Fred slept downstairs with Daddy. They could hear Rebel whimpering in the night in the kennel. So Dad climbed out the window and brought Rebel into the "boys" bedroom. There he spent the night until

Dad returned him to the kennel early in the morning. This went on the whole week of our stay. When Uncle Thompson said goodbye at the end of our visit he said to Dad: “See, Fred, you just have to be firm with your dog.” Daddy smiled and never let on.

Daddy was a social person, especially when he was young. He was not only handsome, he was charming. My cousin Adalene told me, "Your dad was my favorite uncle." "He was the nicest man I ever met," said Mother after he died.

My father was a very knowledgeable man. He was an expert on how things worked and he knew a lot about history. Sometimes we children would ask him a question on these topics. That gave Daddy a chance to expatiate at length on the answer. We got antsy after a few minutes, we didn’t expect so much information! But we were trained to be polite and we didn’t run away or even ask to be excused, we waited on tenterhooks until he finished, then dashed off.

When mother and Daddy bought our house on 4th street in 1956, Daddy’s talent for home repair was in full view. He knocked down a wall; he put in a bathroom. When we lived in the apartment Fred tells me he would fix the toilet and later he even installed a shower in the bathroom. He perched plywood on the molding of the walls of the small hall in our apartment to make shelves for our toys and games. I remember the night I saw Daddy sitting on top of a ladder in the kitchen, his face, hair and clothes bespattered with paint. He was trying out a paint sprayer and the ceiling was a challenge. He wasn’t mad, he looked befuddled, almost comical, he hadn’t factored in gravity.

When he was young my dad started to feel sympathy for black people and Native Americans. He witnessed abuse of these minorities and it turned him around. He was a reader and a thinker and went to college for one year before he left for New York. Despite his political and social differences with his family, he was keenly attached to his siblings, and we visited these relatives many times.

Dad's oldest brother was John, the first born of the second family. He lived in Lexington, Mississippi, the family's home. When John was older he owned a general store in the town. Like many store owners, he extended credit to folks who lacked the funds to pay immediately, mostly black people. Dad told with relish the story of the New Deal extending low-interest loans to individuals. Many black people paid off their credit bills to Uncle John who was not happy about that. The Federal Government had weakened his control in the community

Clarabel was John's daughter, she was a few years older than I, and when I was alone with her she would make racist remarks. "These are the shacks where the 'nigras' live," she said with a sneer as we drove through the outskirts of town. I didn't understand all the implications of her gibes at age nine or ten, but to me there was a chilly, dark cloud hanging over this place in the midst of bright sunshine and heat.

As my brothers and I got older and Dad's alcoholism persisted, we all had our theories as to why Dad could not control his addiction, could not overcome it. I had many thoughts about that: his job as a telephone installer was skilled and must have challenged his talents, but it did not satisfy his deep intelligence. Working for AT&T was not the socially conscious environment he wanted.

Most of all I felt that his deep desire for a relationship with his father had been thwarted by the circumstances of their lives. Maybe he was emulating his father who also drank to excess. In any case, when I entered college and got interested in psychology, I had a pressing desire to help him. I found out about a county clinic that treated "problem drinkers." Daddy respected my opinion as we talked about politics and the problems of the day at dinnertime. I badgered him about getting help, and finally he said, "Okay I'll try a session." The first attempt failed. He said, "I couldn't find the door." He had walked around the building to no avail. I was adamant: "You must go back and try again." He did and this time he found the door and went in for an evaluation. I had high hopes for talking therapy. My dad was intelligent, and I thought if his childhood was discussed profoundly and analyzed he might have an epiphany and see his way out of alcoholic despair. Such idealism was demolished when the doctor at the clinic prescribed Valium to calm him down when he became obstreperous and abusive to my mother when he was drunk. This was 1961 when I was planning a European sojourn with my good friend Lynda. I remember saying to my mother, "I'll cancel my trip and stay home and help with Daddy." At this point Dad would take the Valium only from me. "Oh no you won't!" exclaimed my mother. "This is your adventure, your life to live and you will NOT stay home!"

Thanks to Mother I went on my trip and started the journey of my own life.

Aunt Janet aka Mamie

Aunt Janet's birth name was Mamie Janet. In her childhood in Mississippi she was called Mamie, but when she came to New York with my dad in the 1920s, she was in her early twenties and wanted to be called Janet. Maybe Mamie sounded too Southern and she wanted to fit in in New York City. Later in 1952, when Mamie Eisenhower was the first lady, she went back to Mamie. My aunt had many idiosyncrasies. At age ten, when I went South with Aunt Janet and Uncle Dusty, I could hear how her way of talking, her accent, deepened as we moved in a southerly direction. In Florida her speech was slower than usual and punctuated with lots of "y'alls." When we got to Mississippi the drawl was as a native Mississippian, as she was. No New York influence could be detected after living in that city for twenty-three years. She was at home.

Aunt Janet had a beautiful soprano voice and played the piano with a pearly touch. She read music and also played by ear. She sang with the New York Oratorio, a well-known chorus. When she sang jazz and the popular songs of the day on a local radio station, she was dubbed "The Mississippi Miss." The radio producers liked her accent; they found it charming and allowed her to introduce her songs herself. Years later when I came to study jazz and play the standard tunes, I discovered that I knew a lot of the words of these songs. Not surprising since Janet sang in our living room and we listened to the radio a lot.

Janet composed a song, "Mississippi Moon," that she played and sang often for us. Later I came to have the original manuscript and was pleased to see the jazzy chord changes, the change of time signature from 4/4 to 3/4 in the tune and to see the modern chord voicings she used.

Janet was a large presence in our childhood. She and Dusty, her husband, visited us a lot, all holidays and Sunday dinners in between. Janet and Daddy had a love/hate relationship. Janet was two years older than Dad and they had shared a happy but intense childhood with their many siblings. Their mother died when they were nine and eleven years old. Grandfather was caring but distracted by his drinking problems and money difficulties. Grandfather was a Republican and Janet followed suit. Dad was a liberal Democrat and a strong FDR supporter. This difference caused tensions and arguments, as politics was a big topic of conversation. Their bridge games were contentious with Daddy criticizing Mother's bids and challenging Janet's political views — add alcohol and you get a lot of wrangling. I demurred when it came to learning to play bridge. I did not want to get involved in that kerfuffle.

Aunt Janet was an attractive woman. She and her sisters, Adalene and Ruth had white hair at age thirty-five, but they were youthful and lovely in their appearances and had energy to spare. Janet was a Daughters of the American Revolution member and tried many times to get me interested. I was thirteen or so when she took me to a meeting. I did not resonate with that group of women who seemed stodgy and pretentious to me. But Janet never gave up. When I was an adult she would send me applications to the DAR and note our ancestor on the page: "In case you might be interested…it is valuable to have in later years after we older members of the family have passed on."

Mother tolerated Janet but did not embrace her as a desirable influence in our family. The music, yes, we all loved that, but my mother did not welcome her politics and her trying to steer us children in her direction. When I was seven or so Janet saw me playing in the street with neighborhood children. One boy was African-American. Mother told me years later that Janet came into our apartment all a-flutter. "Sallie is holding hands with a black boy!" We were playing a circle game. Mother and Daddy were not fazed by Janet's observations and prejudices. They wanted us to know and play with children from all backgrounds.

Janet's first husband was Michael Edward Brady, an artist who signed his work MEB. He was known as MEB to his friends. Janet told and retold the story that when he was young MEB was the model for the Dutch Boy Paint logo, the boy on the scaffold with his blond hair and can of paint. MEB died very young and 5 years later Janet married Willis Rhodes, known as Dusty. Uncle Dusty was a photographer for the Journal-American, a New York City newspaper. He was a very good photographer and won prizes for his work. Eventually Dusty opened his own studio in Valley Stream, Long Island. He was a portrait artist and had many clients who were in the public eye. Janet helped out with the clerical aspect of the work. She liked all his clients, especially the "important" ones: the governor of New York, Republicans running for office, the concert pianist, and business people. Janet was a talented person herself, but she also basked in the reflected glory of others. Sometimes Dusty

Sallie and Aunt Janet 1945.

would take a picture of a celebrity that included Janet as someone passing by or standing near. She enjoyed that.

On the other hand, Janet made the normal achievements of her family into huge major events. She and I corresponded when I was an adult and her letters were an accounting of events told in such a way as to magnify the deeds. She had a Norman Vincent Peale "Positive Outlook!" I sent her a picture of the women's rock band I had joined; although she had never met the women or heard us play, she wrote: "The five girls are pretty, charming and have talent! How 'bout a name: The Ragtime Five, Magnolia Quintet, The Melody Maids?" Little did Janet know that most of the women in the band were lesbian, and we played our brand of raunchy rock and roll at the gay clubs in San Francisco!

I appreciated Janet's early musical influence; I ignored her politics and her superficial habit of ascribing importance to titles and people in political office. She framed her invitation to Eisenhower's inauguration. I'm sure all donors received one. My brother Fred remembers that Aunt Janet took such pride in introducing him as "Lieutenant Fred Rhyne" when he was in the Navy.

The last time I saw Janet was in 1989. She was eighty- seven and had dementia. She seemed to recognize my brother Fred, maybe because he had Dad's name. I played her piano in the community room of the facility where she lived. Fred told me she leaned over to him and said, "Oh I like her playing, who is she?"

My Amazing Cousin, John Rison Jones, Jr.

My paternal grandfather was born in Mississippi in 1846. After fighting in the Civil War for the Confederates, he became a cotton farmer in the small town of Lexington, Mississippi. His first wife bore him eight children before she died; his second wife, my grandmother birthed nine more children. The second child was Ruth. She moved to Huntsville, Alabama in her twenties and married John Rison Jones, a wealthy businessman. Ruth convinced her two younger sisters, Lallah and Adalene to move to Huntsville, as there were many well-heeled bachelors in that town. Her sisters took the advice and found husbands in Huntsville. My cousin, John Rison Jones, Jr. was the third child of Ruth and her husband.

When John was thirteen in 1937, he went to Mexico City with family friends. Shortly after arriving, an earthquake destroyed the hotel where they were staying. Fortunately for John the authorities found him a place to stay in the compound of Diego Rivera, the Mexican artist. Leon Trotsky was there too and as a result, John had security clearance problems all his working life. Diego took a liking to John and showed him the art he had made and collected. John's mother had given him $25 to spend on souvenirs. A nascent art collector, John chose to buy a Picasso sketch, a Matisse and several Rivera pieces with his money. People in Huntsville laughed at his souvenirs. "I was supposed to get maracas and sombreros, I guess," he remembered.

After graduating from Huntsville High in 1942, John enlisted in the army. He was assigned to the 104th Infantry Division in Europe. He saw combat and his outfit liberated the slave labor concentration camp, Dora-Mittelbau near Nordhausen in Germany. The experience was devastating and haunted him all his life. Years later in 1987 when John was 63, a holocaust denier, John Irving, was invited to speak at the public library in Huntsville. In the middle of the speech John rose from his seat and called out "You are a liar and a fraud, I was there." This was not John's usual manner, to confront a speaker but he said, "Something came over me during that speech. I was reminded of Elie Wiesel's words:

"For the living and the dead we must bear witness."

In 1994 the temple B'nai Sholom invited John to give a major address during Holocaust Remembrance Week. He did and also spoke at schools and to other groups. A few years later John was honored by the Temple and the Jewish Federation of Huntsville and Northern Alabama in a special commemorative service. He was given a plaque that said:

"John Rison Jones: Liberator, Educator, Friend, promoting interfaith understanding in the Huntsville community." My cousin was very moved by the ceremony and the award. Many friends and family members were in attendance, and he wrote: "I fear that even with such support, I was ready to cry again. In fact I did."

When John came home from the war in 1945, he returned to the segregated South. He wrote: "It didn't make any sense. We went out to rid the world of evil, and we were perpetrating our own evil here at home. And look at our record of treatment of Native Americans. I was one messed up kid. Fortunately I had two wonderful professors at Sewanee College who literally took me apart and put me back together." John graduated from

Sewanee with honors in 1949. He stayed to teach history for two years and then earned a Masters and PhD at the University of North Carolina, Chapel Hill. He was awarded a Fulbright Scholarship and studied at the Sorbonne in Paris where he earned another PhD. At the academic procession in Paris the celebrants wore wide and flowing mauve robes and large broad brimmed hats rather than the mortarboards worn at American universities. John chose to wear the French apparel whenever he was in an academic procession later in life. He called the Paris procession, "The best drag show ever."

In 1960 John joined the faculty at Southern Methodist University in Dallas, Texas, where he taught history. He was the Department Head and directed the Ford Foundation's MA-3 Honors Program. John was doing all he could to integrate the school and finding stubborn resistance. The Ford Foundation was reluctant to give grants to a segregated school so the University bought a black college and added those students to their roster without combining the two populations. John was not happy, but fortunately something unexpected happened.

A happy circumstance changed everything. A male Teaching Assistant in the graduate school seduced him! John was amazed at this turn of events. He had observed the world of gay men surreptitiously in the background of his social life, but he didn't understand it until he discovered his own sexuality.

My brother Fred, a gay man, told me that our aunts Janet and Lillian used to argue about John. Was he homosexual or not? "Who gives a damn," said our father, annoyed by the discussion.

It was a blessing that in the 1960s, John was offered a

Sallie and cousin John — 2002

John's house — 2002

job in Sargeant Shriver's Office of Economic Opportunity in Washington D.C. The objective was to develop the Upward Bound Program for disadvantaged youth. John resigned from Southern Methodist University to accept the federal position. He fled Dallas gladly. He said, "It was the best time to exit stage left with a bow and a kiss." The Queen of the May, as my brother Fred referred to John, was now exiled from the South and became the new kid on the block in the capitol city.

John found his work for the federal government fulfilling and he was catapulted into the social life of gay men in that city. He and a group of lawyer friends organized a network called "Bachelor Lawyers of Washington." (BLOW) They had parties and open houses on holidays and other times. John loved partying, hosting, and attending. In the whirl of gay life in D.C. he was exultant. He told me he had a long-term relationship with the love of his life at that time.

John continued to build his art collection all his life. He added more of the great masters: Rembrandt and Whistler as well as local Alabama talent. He said, "The works I have collected over the years—- these are my children; each one unique and beautiful. They give me joy and good feeling; they are works from the soul and have deep meaning for me as a collector because of the emotion tied to the artist." I was thrilled to see his collection at his home in Huntsville when I visited him in 2001. He had two large Picasso sketches for the great mural Guernica. There was a Matisse painting of circle dancers. In the bathroom, he displayed Russian woodcuts: costumed soldiers in all manner of dance-like positions. John also collected furniture and ceramics. He himself embroidered pettipoint cushions. Where he found time to do that is a mystery.

It seemed to me that my cousin was interested in every aspect of life. He had a vast, hugely encompassing collection of jazz and classical records and CDs. His taste was defined and diverse, but he didn't like Mozart. Once we were talking on the phone, and I said I thought Mozart's music was perfect. "Perfect Hell!" was his response. John was a patron of certain jazz artists before they became famous. Shirley Horn, the pianist and singer was one who received financial help from John as her career got started.

John himself composed music and had a baby grand piano. He showed me the manuscripts when I visited him and I played them. I praised his compositions that he wrote by ear. I told him what chords he had used: "Wow! This is a D flat dominant flat nine chord!" He was pleased. On that visit in 2001, John hosted a party for me to introduce me to thirty cousins, most of whom I had never met or even heard of. He was in his element hosting, introducing, telling stories and cooking. He prepared most of the dinner buffet himself. I watched him in the afternoon at his stove: stirring, sniffing, tasting, then stepping outside to cut herbs from his garden for his creations. John regaled me with information on his plants. He collected seeds and sent me some hosta to plant in my garden; a true renaissance man.

John retired from federal service in 1986. But retired is not a word associated with John Rison Jones. He got involved with the Huntsville Historical Society and other groups. He wrote articles for the Historical Society and published a book on our grandfather's family. His interest in genealogy ran deep.

John was a lifelong smoker and for all his brilliance he found it hard to recognize that this habit was destroying his health. I mentioned to him that his persistent cough had something to do with smoking. "Oh no," he assured me, "it's just post nasal drip." In 2002, he was diagnosed with emphysema. He called it "a mild case." Five years later the doctors insisted he give up smoking, and finally he did. He was proud of himself for resisting the few packs of cigarettes he left around the house "just in case my willpower fails."

A lifelong Democrat and a steadfast advocate for integration, he was overjoyed to have Barack Obama nominated for President in 2008. I hope he knew that Obama won for he died that election morning. He was eighty-four. Sadly he died before he could celebrate Obama's victory.

The Huntsville Times printed John's obituary and quoted Clayton Bass, the President of the Huntsville Museum of Art. " John was like a living encyclopedia. When he passed away he took something with him that was wonderful and profound, and I regret to say, probably irreplaceable." John left his entire art collection to the Huntsville Museum

Lynda

I met Lynda in a freshman math class at Brooklyn College in 1956. We must have started talking in the class, because I remember leaving the class together, continuing a conversation as we walked down the hall. I sensed a kindred spirit, which deepened through the years; we are still friends.

Lynda and I were opposites in several ways. She was a blonde, Slavic beauty with a voluptuous figure; I was a skinny, bespectacled, studious-looking brunette. I wasn't nerdy but I looked that way. I was an optimist, and an idealistic democratic socialist. Lynda was somewhat pessimistic and had no faith in any political philosophy apart from general democracy. She had a very open and vulnerable emotional side that surprised me. My mother was born in Scotland and was rather stoical. She and we children abhorred the lugubrious sentimentality my father displayed when he had been drinking. I ended up being inhibited in the outright expression of feeling. Not so with Lynda. One day she burst into tears as we left our math class after a test. " Oh I did so badly," she moaned, "I probably failed that test!"

"I'm sure you did okay," I said comfortingly, "you're very smart."

The idea of crying over a test was foreign to me.

Lynda had a fascinating personal history. She was born in Poland of Catholic parents in 1938. Her father was an officer in the Polish army. He could not return home after the War, because Polish patriots were regularly arrested and detained by the Russian occupiers. Lynda's father sent in agents to bring his family out of the country.

Lynda — Brooklyn Botanical Gardens 1957

The family was his wife, Lynda, and her brother, George. The first attempt at escape was unsuccessful. The family was not allowed to board the train that would have left Poland. The guards questioned them and tried to scare Lynda, age seven, by approaching her with a German Shepard dog on a leash. They asked about her mother's finances. Lynda, unfazed, responded by petting the dog. She was already an animal lover. The family was put in jail for a few days, Lynda's mother locked in a cell, the children allowed to roam around the building.

On the second attempt, the family walked across a lonely border at night., Lynda wished she had her doll she had left behind. They walked many miles into East Germany where the agent procured false passports for them to enter West Germany and be united with Lynda's father. They lived in England for two years before immigrating to New York City.

I was thrilled by this true story of adventure and danger. The War had made a huge impression on us in Brooklyn. The blackouts, the food rationing, the recycling, and the celebrations at the end were seared into my memory. Lynda had been in the thick of it!

Lynda and I shared a love of plants and animals. She introduced me to cats. Our family and others around us had dogs, and though I liked cats and sympathized greatly with them when I saw neighborhood boys swing them around by their tails. I had never had the pleasure of petting a cat or having one rub up against my leg. Lynda's cat was Picasso, a sleek black and white beauty who allowed Lynda to pick him up and kiss him.

Lynda was my first Buddhist teacher. Neither one of us was aware of Buddha at that time, but the reverence

Lynda and Picasso — 1956

for life Lynda showed was in that tradition. I was sympathetic to pet animals, but insects were a bother. We killed roaches all the time. My friend made me aware that ants and indeed all insects have a right to exist along with us. They were alive and sentient too. This was a deeper level of awareness and I recognized it. One day Lynda dragged me along with her to the college campus pond. "They're cleaning the pond!" she exclaimed. Somehow she knew that when they cleaned the pond, the workers unceremoniously threw the fish out of the water on to the sidewalk walkway surrounding the pond, where they languished and died. I see her in my mind's eye, cupping the small fish in her hands and surreptitiously slipping them back into the water away from the workers. Such kindness endeared her to me.

Lynda and I spent time in the Brooklyn Botanical Gardens, oohing and aahing over flowers. Noses to the roses, we inhaled deeply, our awakening senses stimulated and satisfied. The colors of the garden were riotous in the spring and we exulted in the display. Neither of us had any sexual experience beyond chaste kisses with boys. This was the norm in the 1950s for girls of seventeen-eighteen years of age. We indulged our sensuality in nature, art, and music.

As with all girls of our age, we were concerned about our physical appearance. No one ever measures up. I was too thin and flat-chested; Lynda had breasts that were too large. We bemoaned these facts to each other, and although we were so different, it amounted to the same thing: we were embarrassed by our physique. "I'm like a cow!" Lynda would exclaim. "At least you're womanly," I whimpered feeling so inferior. We were not even interested in boys and relationships; our intellectual and cultural pursuits trumped that. Still we wanted it all.

The Metropolitan Museum of Art in Manhattan had a large impressionist section, and Lynda and I swooned over the works of Monet, Renoir and others. The colors, the softness, the mystical light in these paintings touched our hearts. And we were in love with Leonard Bernstein, the conductor of the New York Philharmonic Orchestra. We went to Carnegie Hall and beyond to see him dance before the orchestra and listen to the lush, melodious sounds he extracted from them. One concert was outdoors at one of the City Colleges. We sat in stadium seats and watched him sitting at the piano, playing and conducting Gershwin's "Rhapsody in Blue." This was heaven for me, a piano player. Bernstein brought such excitement and passion to everything he did. This was life and beauty and truth, and we were exhilarated.

Linda and I reprised our trip to Europe in 2009. This time we just visited France and Italy. We loved it.

Acknowledgements

This book has been a long time coming — over ten years! So many people have helped me and given me support. Thank you all! My brothers, Fred and Bill, spent hours with me reminiscing about Brooklyn and our family. It's what we like to do. My incredible memoir group has been invaluable. Great suggestions, grammatical corrections, chapter titles, and general urging me on. These dear people heard all the chapters at least twice. Muchas gracias amigos.

Marty Conrad was my first reader and gave me excellent advice. Annie, my editor, brought me the title suggested by Sherry, our mutual friend. And Annie gave me some good words, and organized the book. Bravo! At the last minute Pauline urged me to include the Brooklyn Dodgers' stories. Right! My dear friend Paul made the beautiful cover and introduced me to Mark Weiman, the publisher. Thanks Mark! Paul shepherded the book towards publication with his wonderful suggestions and emendations. Many thanks! Many friends read chapters and asked for more. How gratifying! It took a village.

PHOTO GALLERY

Daddy amd Sallie 1940, Prospect Park

Mother and Sallie 1940, Prospect Park

Dress Up 1941

Fred, Sallie, dollhouse made by Daddy 1944

Electra, Oedipus 1946

Fred, Sallie, Mother Coney Island 1946

Powder Puff Dollies
Left: ?, Ann, Sallie

San Francisco Mime Troupe — 1968

Yuk City — Starry Plough 1969

Halloween at Pinel — 1970

Sallie and Lucifer — Berkeley 1975

Sallie and Lynda — Paris 1961

Lynda and Sallie — Paris 2009

CPSIA information can be obtained
at www.ICGtesting.com
Printed in the USA
FSHW020816030222
88099FS

9 781587 905896